中国英雄故事 Stories of
Famous Chinese
Heroes

Published by: The Commercial Press (U.S.) Ltd.
13-17 Elizabeth Street, 2nd Floor
New York, NY 10013

Stories of Famous Chinese Heroes
Intermediate-Advanced READ ABOUT CHINA

Editor: Betty Wong

Printed in Hong Kong

http://www.chinese4fun.net

Contents

目 录

出版说明　Publisher's Note

PUBLISHER'S NOTE

After studying one to two years of Chinese you have also gained the knowledge of quite a bit of vocabulary. You may be wondering whether there are any other ways for you to further improve your Chinese language proficiency? Although there are a lot of books in the market that are written for people who are studying Chinese it is not easy to find an interesting and easy to read book that matches up to one's level of proficiency. You may find the content and the choice of words for some books to be too difficult to handle. You may also find some books to be too easy and the content is too naive for high school students and adults. Seeing the demand for this kind of learning materials we have designed a series of reading materials, which are composed of vivid and interesting content, presented in a multi-facet format. We think this can help students who are learning Chinese to solve the above problem. Through our reading series you can improve your Chinese and at the same time you will learn a lot of Chinese culture.

Our series includes Chinese culture, social aspects of China, famous Chinese literary excerpts, pictorial symbols of

China, famous Chinese heroes…and many other indispensable aspects of China for those who want to really understand Chinese culture. While enjoying the reading materials one can further one's knowledge of Chinese culture from different angles. The content of the series are contextualized according to the wordbase categorization of HSK. We have selected our diction from the pre-intermediate, intermediate to advanced level of Chinese language learners. Our series is suitable for students at the pre-intermediate, intermediate to advanced level of Chinese and working people who are studying Chinese on their own.

The body of our series is composed of literary articles. The terms used in each article are illustrated with the romanised system called Hànyǔ pīnyīn for the ease in learning the pronunciation. Each article has an English translation with explanation of the vocabulary. Moreover there is related background knowledge in Expansion Reading. Interesting games are added to make it fun to learn. We aim at presenting a three-dimensional study experience of learning Chinese for our readers.

Jīng Kē Cì Qínwáng

荆轲刺秦王

Jing Ke's Attempt to Assassinate the King of the State of Qin

Pre-reading Questions

1. In the eyes of the Chinese, what kind of people will be counted as losers?

2. The assassins in ancient China did not murder for money. Can you make a guess as to their motives for committing murder?

---

❶ Èr qiān duō nián qián, Zhōngguó réngrán shì Zhànguó
二 千 多 年 前, 中国 仍然 是 战国
shídài dànshì Qínguó yǐjing hěn qiángdà kuài yào miè diào
时代, 但是 秦国 已经 很 强大, 快 要 灭 掉
qítā dà guó Nà shíhou Zhōngguó yǒu hěn duō xiáshì¹ tāmen
其他 大 国。 那 时候, 中国 有 很 多 侠士¹, 他们
wǔgōng gāoqiáng zhǐyào yǒu rén xīnshǎng tāmen jiù kěyǐ wèi
武功 高强, 只要 有 人 欣赏 他们, 就 可以 为
nàge rén zuòshì jiùshì sǐ yě bù pà
那个 人 做事, 就是 死 也 不 怕。

❷ Jīng Kē jiùshì zhèyàng de xiáshì Dāngshí Yānguó dǎ
荆 轲 就是 这样 的 侠士。 当时 燕国 打
bù guò Qínguó bèi Qínguó duó qu hěn duō tǔdì Yānguó
不 过 秦国, 被 秦国 夺 去 很 多 土地。 燕国

de tàizǐ jiàozuò Yān Dān tā duì Jīng Kē hěn hǎo yào
的 太子 叫做 燕丹，他 对 荆 轲 很 好，要

shénme gěi shénme Tā xīwàng Jīng Kē bàn shǐzhě qù
什么 给 什么。 他 希望 荆 轲 扮 使者 去

jiàn Qínwáng wēixié Qínguó jiāo huán tǔdì Rúguǒ Qínwáng
见 秦王，威胁 秦国 交 还 土地。 如果 秦王

bù dāying jiù shā sǐ tā Jīng Kē mǎshàng dāying tā
不 答应，就 杀 死 他，荆 轲 马上 答应，他

shuō Bùguò xiān yào ràng Qínwáng xiāngxìn wǒ shì qù qiúhé²
说："不过，先 要 让 秦王 相信 我 是 去 求和²

de zhèyàng cái néng jiējìn tā Tā zhīdao Qínwáng xiǎng
的，这样 才 能 接近 他。" 他 知道 秦王 想

dé dào Yānguó zuì féiwò³ de yī kuài tǔdì érqiě xiǎng
得 到 燕国 最 肥沃³ 的 一 块 土地，而且 想

shā sǐ chóurén Fán Wūjī jiāngjūn Yúshì tā xiàng tàizǐ Dān
杀 死 仇人 樊 于期 将军。 于是 他 向 太子 丹

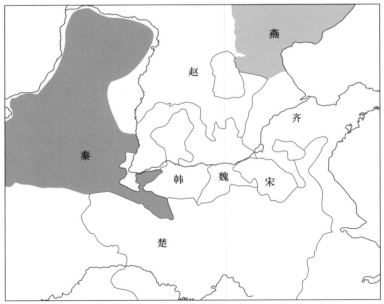

Map of the State of Qin and the State of Yan

提出：“如果我拿着樊将军的头和那块
土地的地图去献给秦王，他一定会接见
我。这样，我就可以对付他了。”太子
丹感到为难，说：“樊将军受秦国迫害才
来找我，我怎能伤害他呢？”于是，荆
轲亲自去找樊于期，告诉他行刺秦王
的计划，然后说：“为了让秦王接见
我，我要借你的头去献给他。”樊于期
说：“好，那你就拿去吧！”说完就拔剑
自杀了。

GLOSSARY

1 侠士　chivalrous warrior　　2 求和　seek peace
3 肥沃　fertile

Translation

❶　　About one to two thousand years ago, China was still in the
Warring States period. But the State of Qin had already become
very strong. It was about to defeat and annex all the other big states.
During that time in China there were a lot of chivalrous warriors, who
were very skillful in martial arts. If they felt enough loyalty to someone
they would work for that person even though the job might cost them

their lives. They were not afraid to die in order to prove their loyalty.

❷ Jing Ke was one of these chivalrous warriors. At that time the State of Yan was losing many battles to the State of Qin and a lot of her land had been taken away by the State of Qin. The prince of the State of Yan was called Prince Dan. He treated Jing Ke very well and gave him whatever he wanted. He wanted Jing Ke to pretend to be a diplomat in order to go see the King of Qin. At the meeting, Jing Ke was to hold the King as a hostage in order to demand the return of the Yan territories taken by the State of Qin. If the King of Qin refused, Jing Ke was to kill him. Without any hesitation Jing Ke promised Prince Dan that he would do this for him and he said, "I will do this. But in order to get close to the King of Qin I have to gain his confidence so that he will believe that I am going to see him for the purpose of seeking peace." He knew that the King of Qin wanted to get possession of the most fertile piece of land that belonged to the State of Yan and he also wanted to kill his personal enemy, General Fan Wuji. He then suggested this to Prince Dan saying, "If I offer both the head of General Fan Wuji and the map of the most fertile land of Yan to the King of Qin as tributes from us, then the King of Qin would definitely grant me a personal interview. Then I could deal with him as planned." Prince Dan felt that it was a very difficult decision and said to Jing Ke, "General Fan Wuji came to me for refuge from the oppression of the King of Qin. How can I hurt him?" Then Jing Ke personally looked for General Fan Wuji and arranged a meeting with him in order to tell him the plan for assassinating the King of Qin. He said to the General, "In order to obtain a personal interview from the King of Qin I have to borrow your head and offer it as a tribute."General Fan Wuji said, "That is a good idea. You can take it now!" After saying this he took out his knife and killed himself.

❸ 荆轲知道这次去秦国，不可能活着回来。太子丹和燕国的大臣在河边为他送行。太子丹给荆轲一把有毒短刀，又给他一个助手。这个助手只有十多岁，已经杀过很多人。荆轲喝过送别的酒，立即出发去秦国。

❹ 秦王听说燕国使者带了樊于期的头和地图来，十分高兴。他决定接见荆轲。荆轲捧着装人头的盒子，年青的助手捧着地图，走上宫殿，没有想到，这个年青的助手怕得发抖。秦王的大臣问："使者为什么发抖？"荆轲没有紧张，他对秦王说："这个年青人从来没见过大王的威严，所以害怕。请大王原谅。"秦王于是要荆轲献上地图。秦王打开卷起来的地图时，预先

cáng zài dìtú li de yǒu dú duǎn dāo lù chulai Jīng Kē
藏 在 地 图 里 的 有 毒 短 刀 露 出 来 。 荆 轲

liánmáng yòng zuǒshǒu lā zhu Qínwáng de xiùzi yòushǒu zhuā qi
连 忙 用 左 手 拉 住 秦 王 的 袖 子 ，右 手 抓 起

duǎn dāo cì xiàng Qínwáng Qínwáng xià le yī tiào yònglì
短 刀 刺 向 秦 王 。 秦 王 吓 了 一 跳 ，用 力

zhēngzhá bǎ xiùzi zhēng duàn le
挣 扎 ，把 袖 子 挣 断 了 。

Translation

❸   Jing Ke knew that he would never be able to survive this mission to the State of Qin. Prince Dan and the high-ranking government ministers gathered beside the riverbank to bid Jing Ke farewell. Prince Dan gave Jing Ke a poisonous short knife and an assistant. This assistant was only a teenage boy but he had already killed many people. After drinking the wine of farewell Jing Ke immediately headed for the State of Qin.

❹   When the King of Qin heard that a Yan diplomat had brought with him the head of General Fan Wuji and the map he was so happy that he decided to grant Jing Ke an interview. Jing Ke was holding the box that contained the head and the young assistant was holding the map. No one could anticipate that the young assistant was so scared that he began to shiver when walking up to the palace. A high-ranking minister of Qin asked, "Why is this diplomat shivering?" Jing Ke did not become excited and said to the King of Qin, "This young man has never seen the dignified majesty of your Highness and this is why he is scared. Please forgive him." Then the King of Qin demanded that Jing Ke offer the map to him. When the King of Qin unfolded the rolled up map the poisonous short knife, which had been planted there before, appeared. Jing Ke immediately held on to the sleeve of the King of Qin with his left hand and used his right hand to grab the short knife to stab him. The King of Qin was shocked and struggled so fiercely that the sleeve broke.

❺ 秦王 想 拔 出 宝剑，可是 他 心 里
着急，剑 又 太 长，拔 不 出来。 虽然
旁边 有 很 多 官员，可是 他们 都 不 能 带
武器。 没有 秦王 的 命令，宫殿 外 的 士兵
又 不 能 进 宫殿。 一时间，人人 都 不 知道
怎么 办 才 好。 秦王 急 得 绕着 宫殿 的
柱子 跑，荆 轲 在 后头 紧 追 着。 官员
只好 大声 喊："大王 拔
宝剑！大王 拔 宝剑！"

❻ 在 危急 关头，一
个 伺候 秦王 的
医生，把 装 药 的
袋子 用力 扔 向
荆 轲。 就 在 荆
轲 挡 开 药 袋 的
时候，秦王 得 到

The King of the State of Qin escaped from an
assassination attempt. Later on he became
the first Emperor of China – Qinshihuang

7

時间 拔 出 宝剑，他 回头 冲 向 荆 轲，砍 断
他 的 左腿。荆 轲 倒 在 地 上，忍 着 痛，用
尽 全 身 力气，把 短 刀 掷⁴ 向 秦王。秦王
一 躲，短 刀 从 他 身边 飞 过，打 中
柱子。秦王 见 荆 轲 没有 武器，拼命 刺
他。荆 轲 知道 自己 已经 失败，靠 在 柱子
上 骂："我 行刺⁵ 失败，因为 我 本来 想 抓 住
你，逼 你 交还 土地，所以 才 没有 及早 杀
你。"秦国 的 官员 冲 上来 杀 死 了 他。

❼　秦王 十分 生气，派 兵 去 打 燕国，终于
把 燕国 灭 了。这个 秦王 后来 成为 中国 的
第 一 个 皇帝 —— 秦始皇。

GLOSSARY

4 掷　　throw
5 行刺　assassinate

Translation

❺ The King of Qin wanted to draw his precious sword. But he was too tensed up by this anxiety and the sword was too long. He could not draw it out. Although there were a lot of government ministers on each side of the room they were never allowed to carry any weapons. Without an order from the King of Qin the soldiers outside the palace could not enter the palace either. At this moment of crisis nobody knew what to do. The King of Qin was so hard pressed that he ran around a pillar trying to escape from Jing Ke who was closely chasing after him. The government ministers of Qin could only shout loudly, "Your Highness! Draw your precious sword! Your Highness! Draw your precious sword!"

❻ At this critical moment, a doctor who was attending to the King of Qin used his bag containing medicines to throw it heavily at Jing Ke. Using the moment of opportunity when Jing Ke blocked the medicine bag, the King of Qin drew his precious sword. He turned around to charge at Jing Ke and cut off his left leg. Jing Ke fell on the ground. Bearing the pain he used the strength of his whole body to throw the short knife at the King of Qin, who shifted aside and the short knife flew right past him. Seeing that Jing Ke was not armed anymore the King of Qin stabbed him as it was a matter of life and death. Jing Ke knew that he had failed. He leaned against the pillar and scolded the King of Qin saying, "My assassination failed because originally I wanted to capture you and hold you as a hostage in order to demand the return of land to the State of Yan. That is why I did not take that earlier opportunity to kill you." The government ministers of Qin charged up to the pillar and killed Jing Ke.

❼ The King of Qin was very angry and sent his army to attack the State of Yan. Finally he annihilated the State of Yan and became the first Emperor of China – Qinshihuang .

The Assassins in Ancient China

There were a lot of famous assassins in ancient China. Most of them were fast and highly skilled in martial arts and extremely loyal to their commitment to the principle of justice and the masters they were serving. There was one who held the king of the enemy country hostage to demand the return of the land that once belonged to his country. He was trying to preserve the national integrity of his nation. There was another one who had been entrusted to kill a high-ranking minister but he found out that this minister was very loyal to his own country. He could not harden his heart enough to kill someone who shared his strong belief in loyalty. Yet without murdering him he could not accomplished his mission. Finally he chose to kill himself to avoid the dilemma. There was another assassin who promised to carry out an assassination mission in return for a favor bestowed on him. He made two attempts to assassinate the targeted person. To disguise himself he put tattoo painting on his face and swallowed smoldered pieces of charcoal to burn his vocal chords so that his voice could not be recognized.

These assassins usually killed in order to achieve a certain political purpose. To accomplish their missions they would sacrifice anything, including their own lives. These assassins are different from the hired murderers of today. Modern day hired-killers work under organized crime associations. They have undergone strict training programs. They regard murdering someone as their occupation. Under the premise of self-preservation is survival, they will kill anyone without asking any questions, provided they are paid enough money.

GAMES FOR FUN

1. On the brick pictures please identify Jing Ke, Qinshihuang , and the poisonous short knife (dagger) being thrown out.

2. Please outline Jing Ke in red.

Qinshihuang   dagger   Jing Ke

Answer:

^{Xiàng Yǔ} ^{pò fǔ chén zhōu}

项羽 —— 破釜沉舟

Xiang Yu – Breaking the Cooking Caldrons and Sinking the Boats to Ensure Victory

Pre-reading Questions

1. In ancient China weight-lifting was also practiced as a form of training. Can you guess how much weight this martial arts hero could lift?

2. Are you surprised to learn that a general ordered his soldiers to smash up all the cooking utensils right before they are going to engage in battle? Why is he doing this?

---

❶
Shéi néng dǎbài Qínshǐhuáng shǒu xià de míngjiàng Jiùshì
谁 能 打败 秦始皇 手 下 的 名将？ 就是

Xiàng Yǔ
项 羽。

❷
Xiàng Yǔ shēncái hěn gāo lìqi hěn dà nénggòu jǔ
项 羽 身材 很 高， 力气 很 大， 能够 举

qǐ jǐ bǎi jīn zhòng de dōngxi Tā shì nánfāng yī gè dà
起 几 百 斤 重 的 东西。 他 是 南方 一 个 大

guó de guìzú[1] hòulái nàge guójiā bèi Qínshǐhuáng xiāomiè
国 的 贵族[1]， 后来 那个 国家 被 秦始皇 消灭

le Qínshǐhuáng yǒu le zhème dà de guójiā xǐhuan
了。 秦始皇 有 了 这么 大 的 国家， 喜欢

到处 去 看看，有 一 次 到 了
dàochù qù kànkan yǒu yī cì dào le

南方，年轻 的 项 羽 和 叔叔
nánfāng niánqīng de Xiàng Yǔ hé shūshu

看见 秦始皇 很 有 气派 的
kànjian Qínshǐhuáng hěn yǒu qìpài de

队伍，他 对 叔叔 说："我 以后
duìwu tā duì shūshu shuō Wǒ yǐhòu

可以 取代 他。" 这 话 吓 了 他 的
kěyǐ qǔdài tā Zhè huà xià le tā de

Portrait of Xiang Yu

叔叔 一 跳，马上 喝 住 他："别 乱 说，要 杀
shūshu yī tiào mǎshàng hè zhu tā Bié luàn shuō yào shā

头 的！" 叔叔 知道 项 羽 有 大志。
tóu de Shūshu zhīdao Xiàng Yǔ yǒu dàzhì

GLOSSARY

1 贵族 nobles

Translation

❶   Who could defeat the famous generals under Qinshihuang's command? The answer was Xiang Yu.

❷   Xiang Yu had a tall stature and he was so strong that he could lift things as heavy as a few hundred catties. He was an aristocrat in a major southern state. Later on that state was annihilated by Qinshihuang, who liked to visit here and there after he had taken possession of such a big country. Once he went to the south. When young Xiang Yu and his uncle saw the majestic troops of Qinshihuang, Xiang Yu said to his uncle, "Later on I can replace him." Taken aback by what he had heard, his uncle immediately shouted at him to stop him from talking anymore and he said, "Don't talk nonsense. Saying things like that will get you beheaded!" His uncle knew that Xiang Yu had a big and ambitious plan for his life.

❸ 后来，秦始皇 突然 死去，他 的 儿子 做 了 皇帝，但是 秦二世 没有 秦始皇 的 能力，天下 大 乱。本来 二 十 多 年 前 被 秦始皇 灭掉 的 国家，重新 反对 秦国。当时 秦国 的 兵力 还是 很 强，秦国 派 三 十 万 大 军 包围 了 赵国，赵国 只好 求救[2]。项 羽 知道 后，立即 说："我 愿意 带 兵 去 救。"可是 因为 项 羽 年轻，他 只 能 做 副 将军。将军 带 着 二 十 万 军队 去 救 赵国，半路 停 了 下来，一直 过 了 四 十 六 天，都 没有 再 前进。因为 将军 怕 打 不 过 秦军，他 想 让 秦军 和 赵军 先 交战[3]，等 秦军 打 得 累 了，再 出 兵。项 羽 反对 将军 的 做法，认为 赵军 实在 太 弱 了，不 会 对 秦军 有 任何 影响，但 将军 不 听。因为 军队 在 路 上 停留 的 时间 太

cháng liángshi yǐjing bù gòu jiā shang tiānqì zhuǎn lěng shìbīng
长 ，粮食 已经 不 够，加 上 天气 转 冷 ，士兵

yòu dòng yòu è dōu mányuàn qilai Xiàng Yǔ zài jūn zhōng
又 冻 又 饿，都 埋怨 起来。项 羽 在 军 中

hěn dé rén xīn jiàn shìbīng dōu yuànyì zuòzhàn biàn shā le
很 得 人 心，见 士兵 都 愿意 作战 ，便 杀 了

jiāngjūn Shìbīng lìjí yōnghù Xiàng Yǔ wéi jiāngjūn biǎoshì
将军。士兵 立即 拥护 项 羽 为 将军 ，表示

yuànyì fúcóng mìnglìng jìnjūn zuòzhàn
愿意 服从 命令 进军 作战 。

GLOSSARY

2 求救 ask for help   3 交战 fight in wars

Translation

❸   Later on Qinshihuang died suddenly and his son became the new Emperor, called Qin'ershi. He did not have the ability of his father and the country was thrown into great chaos. The states annihilated by Qinshihuang over 20 years ago began their rebellion anew against the Qin Empire. At that time the Imperial Army of Qin was still very strong. An Imperial Army of 300,000 soldiers was sent to surround the State of Zhao, which could only send out signals, begging for help from the other states. Knowing this Xiang Yu immediately said, " I am willing to lead an army to go to help them." But because of his young age he could only be assigned the position of an auxiliary general. An army of 200,000 soldiers led by a general was sent to help the State of Zhao. It stopped half way and did not advance any further for over 46 days because the general was afraid that he could not defeat the Imperial Army of Qin. He wanted the fighting between the Zhao and the Qin to tire out the Imperial Army of Qin. Then he would send his army to take advantage of the situation. Xiang Yu objected to this strategic plan. The opinion he voiced was that the army of the State of Zhao was in reality too weak to be able to have any wearing out effects on the Imperial Army. But the general refused to listen to him. Because the army had stayed too long half way there the food supply was getting scarce. In addition the weather turned cold. Hungry and cold the soldiers began to complain. Xiang Yu was very popular in the army and he saw that the soldiers wanted to fight instead of idling there. He therefore killed the general and the soldiers all immediately supported him in unison to be the new eneral. They all expressed their willingness to obey his orders to advance in order to engage in battle.

❹
Xiàng Yǔ xiān pài rén dài sān wàn bīng dǎbài
项 羽 先 派 人 带 三 万 兵 打败

Qínjūn zhànlǐng le héliú Jiēzhe Xiàng Yǔ zhǐhuī dà duì
秦军，占领 了 河流。 接着，项 羽 指挥 大 队

rénmǎ guò hé Děng jūnduì shàng le àn Xiàng Yǔ mìnglìng
人 马 过 河。 等 军队 上 了 岸，项 羽 命令

bǎ chuán quánbù záochén bùdàn rúcǐ hái jiào shìbīng zhǐ
把 船 全部 凿沉， 不但 如此， 还 叫 士兵 只

dài shang sān tiān de liángshi ránhòu bǎ zuò fàn yòng de
带 上 三 天 的 粮食，然后， 把 做 饭 用 的

guō quánbù zásuì⁴ biǎoshì zuòzhàn de juéxīn Xiàng Yǔ
锅 全部 砸碎⁴， 表示 作战 的 决心。 项 羽

dà shēng duì shìbīng
大 声 对 士兵

shuō Nǐmen kàn
说：" 你们 看，

wǒmen yǐjing méiyǒu
我们 已经 没有

hòulù le zài sān
后路 了，在 三

tiān nèi zhǐyǒu dǎ
天 内，只有 打

Xiang Yu ordered the army to sink their boats

shèngzhàng cái néng huó zhe huíqu
胜仗，才能活着回去。

Yīqǐ qiánjìn bù néng tuì
一起 前进，不能退！"

shìbīng gè gè dà shēng hūhǎn
士兵个个大声呼喊，

juéxīn xuèzhàn dàodǐ
决心血战到底。

"Fu, a cauldron" is a cooking utensil
used in ancient China

❺ Yī gè Qínguó de jiāngjūn tīng shuō Xiàng Yǔ
一个秦国的将军听说项羽

pòfǔchénzhōu jiù xiào tā bù dǒng bīngfǎ lián tuìlù dōu
破釜沉舟，就笑他不懂兵法，连退路[5]都

bù gěi zìjǐ liú yī tiáo Nǎli xiǎngdào yīnwèi Qínjūn
不给自己留一条。哪里想到，因为秦军

tài qiángdà Xiàng Yǔ míngbai yīdìng yào xià bì sǐ de
太强大，项羽明白一定要下必死的

juéxīn cái yǒu kěnéng dǎbài Qínjūn Míngjiàng Zhāng Hán
决心，才有可能打败秦军。名将章邯

dài zhe jiǔ duì Qínjūn tā duì shìbīng shuō Xiān yǐn Xiàng
带着九队秦军，他对士兵说："先引项

Yǔ guòlai ránhòu jiǔ duì yīqí bāowéi shangqu Xiàng Yǔ
羽过来，然后九队一齐包围上去，项羽

běnlǐng zài dà yě zǒu bù liǎo Zhànshì kāishǐ Xiàng
本领再大，也走不了。"战事开始，项

Yǔ qí zhe mǎ gēnběn bù pà Qínjūn de bāowéi nǎli
羽骑着马，根本不怕秦军的包围，哪里

Qínbīng duō jiù wǎng nǎli chōng jiāng Qínbīng shā de
秦兵多，就往哪里冲，将秦兵杀得

rényǎngmǎfān sǐ shāng wú shù Xiàng Yǔ de shìbīng yě wú
人仰马翻，死伤无数。项羽的士兵也无

bù yǐ yī dāng shí bǎ Qínjūn shā de dà bài Dāngshí
不以一当十，把秦军杀得大败。当时

gè	guó	de	jūnduì	běnlái	dōu	hàipà	Qínjūn	bù	gǎn
各	国	的	军队	本来	都	害怕	秦军 ,	不	敢

cānjiā	zuòzhàn	kànjian	Xiàng	Yǔ	nàme	yǒnggǎn	dōu
参加	作战 ,	看见	项	羽	那么	勇敢 ,	都

hěn	pèifú	Hòulái	Xiàng	Yǔ	dǎbài	le	Qínguó	suǒyǒu
很	佩服 。	后来	项	羽	打败	了	秦国	所有

jūnduì	zhànlǐng	le	Qín	de	shǒudū
军队 ,	占领	了	秦	的	首都 。

GLOSSARY

4 砸碎　break into pieces　　　5 退路　leave a way open for retreat

Translation

❹　　To begin the war against the Imperial Army, Xiang Yu sent someone to lead an army of 30,000 soldiers to fight the Qin Army and they occupied the river. Then Xiang Yu directed the rest of the large army to cross the river. After the whole army had landed on the other side he ordered the soldiers to chisel holes in the bottoms of all the boats to sink them. Moreover he ordered the soldiers to carry with them three days of food supply. To show their determination to fight he then ordered that all the cooking caldrons be smashed. In a loud voice he told the soldiers, "Look! We do not have any way of retreat. We have to win our war in three days in order to stay alive to return home. We have to advance together. No one can retreat!" Each and every soldier shouted back in a loud voice too to show their determination to fight the war to the end with their blood if they had to. One of the generals of the Imperial Army heard of Xiang Yu's decision to break all the cooking caldrons and sink all the boats and he was secretly laughing at Xiang Yu, thinking that he did not know anything about military tactics. He did not even leave a way open for retreat. He could not imagine the difficulty facing Xiang Yu, who knew very well that in order to defeat the Imperial Army of Qin, which was in reality too strong for his army, his soldiers had to have the determination to fight in spite of the strong possibility of certain death.

❺   The famous Qin general Zhang Han was leading and commanding nine armies and he said to his soldiers," First we will lure Xiang Yu to advance deep into our area and then all nine armies will go to surround him. No matter how strong his power is he can never escape." The battle began. Riding his horse, Xiang Yu basically did not have any fear of the surrounding tactics of the Qin armies. He charged wherever there were a lot of the Qin soldiers, killing many of them. Fallen soldiers and horses were everywhere. Xiang Yu's soldiers too were so brave that each fought as if he were fighting against ten Qin soldiers. The Imperial Army of Qin was totally defeated. During that time all the various other states' armies were originally too afraid of the Qin army to join the war against the Qin Empire. Seeing Xiang Yu's brave performance they all admired him. Later on Xiang Yu defeated all of the Qin armies and occupied the capital of the Qin Empire.

The River of Chu and the Boundary Line of Han on the Chessboard of Chinese Chess

The Japanese game of "Go" is the ancient Chinese chess game. But nowadays Chinese chess is the chess game played by the majority of chess players. The chess pieces are divided into two groups, each group has 16 pieces in its individual colour (two colours in total). The chessboard of Chinese chess is divided into a network, formed by the crossing of nine longitudinal lines by ten horizontal ones. The chess pieces move along the crossing points of the network of lines. Historically, Chinese chess is a game that came to China from India. But the line of division on the chessboard dividing the two chess players has a Chinese story. The central space sandwiched by the two horizontal lines does not have any longitudinal lines. This narrow space is called the "river boundary", on which four Chinese characters "Chu He Han Jie" are usually written. The four chracters mean "The River of Chu and the

Boundary line of Han". This "river boundary" is related to a story about Xiang Yu.

The term, "Chu He Han Jie, meaning the River of Chu and the Boundary line of Han", originates from Hong Gou. Hong Gou is a canal in ancient China. Xiang Yu used a lot of effort to defeat the army of the State of Qin. But Liu Bang took possession of the capital of the State of Qin, occupying it earlier than Xiang Yu. Then a war broke out between the two and it lasted for several years. This war has been called the Struggle for Supremacy between the State of Chu and the State of Han (205 B. C. to 202 B. C.). There was a treaty between Liu Bang and Xiang Yu. The treaty stated that the territories west of Hong Gou belonged to Liu Bang and his State of Chu. The land east of Hong Gou was part of Xiang Yu's territories. Then Hong Gou was called the River of Chu and the Boundary line of Han. On modern maps Hong Gou is located at the City of Xing Yang in He Nan Province. The opening of this canal is approximately 800 meters wide and 200 meters deep.

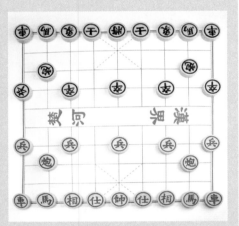

The middle division (The River of Chu and the Boundary line of Han) on the chessboard of the Chinese chess comes from the historical story of a state boundary settlement between Liu Bang and his rival, Xiang Yu

Sū Wǔ mùyáng

苏武牧羊

Su Wu, the Loyal Diplomat Shepherd

Pre-reading Questions

1. Unexpectedly, a diplomat in ancient China suddenly became a shepherd. What was the reason?

2. Is the chance of survival high for a person subsisting only on a diet of drinking water from melted snow and eating animal fur?

---

❶

Gōngyuán qián   nián   shì Zhōngguó de
公元 前 100 年，是 中国 的

Hàn cháo   Zhège   shíhou   Zhōngguó běifāng
汉 朝。 这个 时候，中国 北方

yǒu gè   mínzú   jiào Xiōngnú   Hàn
有 个 民族 叫 匈奴。 汉

cháo hé Xiōngnú   zhī   jiān   jīngcháng
朝 和 匈奴 之 间 经常

fāshēng zhànzhēng   Hàn cháo huángdì
发生 战争。 汉 朝 皇帝

wèi   le   biǎoshì   yǒuhǎo   pài   le
为 了 表示 友好， 派 了

yī gè jiào zuò Sū Wǔ de wàijiāo
一 个 叫 做 苏 武 的 外交

Su Wu, the diplomat who tended sheep

guānyuán ná zhe dàibiǎo Hàn cháo shǐzhě de jiézhàng qù
官员，拿着代表汉朝使者的节杖去
Xiōngnú nàli Sū Wǔ qù dào cǎoyuán hòu Xiōngnú zú
匈奴那里。苏武去到草原后，匈奴族
li fāshēng le wángzǐ bèipàn guójiā de shìqing Sū Wǔ
里发生了王子背叛国家的事情。苏武
yǒu yī gè zhùshǒu jiào Zhāng Shèng yǔ bèipàn de rén shì
有一个助手叫张胜，与背叛的人是
hǎo péngyou suǒyǐ yě bèi zhuā qilai Xiōngnúwáng yào Hàn
好朋友，所以也被抓起来。匈奴王要汉
cháo shǐzhě tóuxiáng Sū Wǔ bù yuànyì tā duì yīqǐ
朝使者投降。苏武不愿意，他对一起
lái de rén shuō Rúguǒ tóuxiáng le wǒmen bùdàn méiyǒu
来的人说："如果投降了，我们不但没有
wánchéng shǐmìng hái lìng guójiā xiūrǔ Jiù suàn néng huó
完成使命[1]，还令国家羞辱[2]。就算能活
xialai wǒmen yòu zěnme yǒu liǎn huí zǔguó ne Shuō
下来，我们又怎么有脸回祖国呢？"说
wán jiù bá chū dāo lái zìshā dàn bèi tóngbàn jiù le
完就拔出刀来自杀，但被同伴救了
guòlai
过来。

GLOSSARY

1 使命 mission
2 羞辱 humiliation

Translation

❶   In 100 B.C. during the Han Dynasty there was a tribe, called Xiongnu, in northern China. Wars frequently broke out between the Han and the Xiongnu. To show a gesture of friendliness the Han Emperor sent a diplomat, called Su Wu, to visit the Xiongnu. Carrying the scepter which represented the envoy of the Han Government, Su Wu went to the grasslands where the Xiongnu lived. After his arrival there was an incident of a Xiongnu prince committing a crime of treason against his own country. Su Wu had an assistant, called Zhang Sheng, who was a good friend of this traitor. He was therefore arrested too. The Xiongnu King ordered the Han diplomat to surrender. Su Wu did not want to do so. He said to those people who accompanied him on the mission, "By surrendering not only shall we leave our mission unfinished but also our country will feel ashamed of us. Although we can save our lives how can we keep our dignity when we return to our home country?" After saying this he took out his knife to kill himself. But he was saved by his fellow companions.

❷

Xiōngnúwáng	zhīdao	le	hěn	xīnshǎng	Sū	Wǔ
匈奴王	知道	了,	很	欣赏	苏	武

de	pǐndé	tā	bùduàn	de	xiǎng	bànfǎ	bī	Sū	Wǔ
的	品德,	他	不断	地	想	办法	逼	苏	武

tóuxiáng	Yǒu	yī	cì	tā	ràng	yī	gè	tóuxiáng	Xiōngnú
投降。	有	一	次,	他	让	一	个	投降	匈奴

de	Hàn	cháo	guānyuán	qù	quàn	Sū	Wǔ	Zhège	guānyuán	ná
的	汉	朝	官员	去	劝	苏	武。	这个	官员	拿

zhe	dāo	wēixié	shuō	Zhāng	Shèng	yào	shāhài	guówáng	xìnrèn
着	刀	威胁	说:"	张	胜	要	杀害	国王	信任

de	dàchén	yīnggāi	chǔsǐ	Rúguǒ	nǐmen	tóuxiáng	wǒ
的	大臣,	应该	处死。	如果	你们	投降,	我

jiù	bù	shā	nǐmen	Zhāng	Shèng	xià	de	mǎshàng	jiù	tóuxiáng
就	不	杀	你们。"	张	胜	吓	得	马上	就	投降

了。官员又对苏武说："张胜是你的同伴，他犯罪，你也要受惩罚。"可是苏武不怕威胁，说："我根本没有杀匈奴人的想法，我又不是张胜的亲人，为什么要为他犯的罪接受惩罚？"官员见到只是威胁不能成功，又说："我投降匈奴以后，国王把我当作兄弟，让我做官，送给我很多牛羊和钱。如果你投降了，你也会过上这样的生活。你不投降，就要被杀掉。"苏武生气地骂他："你背叛³了国家，当了敌国的大臣，还想让我学你吗？其他国家杀汉朝的使者，汉朝会报复。如果我死了，那么匈奴就会有大祸⁴了！"

A scepter was the symbol of the execution of an order from the Emperor

❸ Xiōngnúwáng tīng dào
匈奴王 听 到

zhège huídá jiù gèng
这个 回答， 就 更

xīwàng Sū Wǔ tóuxiáng Tā
希望 苏 武 投降。 他

bǎ Sū Wǔ guān zài láofáng
把 苏 武 关 在 牢房

The Baikal Lake, shaped like an ecliptic moon, is long, narrow and looped-shaped

zhōng bù gěi tā shíwù
中， 不 给 他 食物

hé shuǐ Tiān xiàxuě le Sū Wǔ jiù kào hē xuěshuǐ
和 水。 天 下雪 了， 苏 武 就 靠 喝 雪水

hé chī jiézhàng shang de máopí wéichí shēngmìng Guò le
和 吃 节杖 上 的 毛皮 维持 生命。 过 了

jǐ tiān Xiōngnú rén fāxiàn Sū Wǔ hái méi sǐ dōu hěn
几 天， 匈奴 人 发现 苏 武 还 没 死， 都 很

jīngyà Tāmen rènwéi Sū Wǔ shì shénrén Xiōngnúwáng
惊讶。 他们 认为 苏 武 是 神人。 匈奴王

bǎ Sū Wǔ dāndú dài dào hěn yuǎn hěn yuǎn de
把 苏 武 单独 带 到 很 远 很 远 的

Běihǎi jīntiān Xībólìyà de Bèijiā'ěr Hú ràng tā
北海（ 今天 西伯利亚 的 贝加尔湖）， 让 他

sìyǎng gōng yáng bìng xiàlìng yào děng gōng yáng shēng chu le xiǎo
饲养 公 羊， 并 下令 要 等 公 羊 生 出 了 小

yáng cái néng ràng tā huílai Zhè qíshí jiùshì yào bǎ Sū
羊 才 能 让 他 回来。 这 其实 就是 要 把 苏

Wǔ qiújìn qilai
武 囚禁[5] 起来。

GLOSSARY

3 背叛 betray

4 祸 disaster

5 囚禁 keep somebody in captivity

Translation

❷   Learning this, the Xiongnu King greatly appreciated Su Wu's moral ethic. Incessantly he tried many ways to force Su Wu to surrender. Once he let a former Han government officer, who had surrendered to the Xiongnu, convince Su Wu to do the same. This former Han government officer used a knife to threaten Zhang Sheng and Su Wu. He said to them, "Zhang Sheng wanted to kill the high-ranking government minister whom the Xiongnu King trusted very much. This is a crime punishable by execution. If both of you surrender I will not kill you both." Zhang Sheng was so scared that he surrendered immediately. Then this former Han government officer said to Su Wu, "Zhang Sheng is your companion. He has committed a crime. You have to be punished too." But Su Wu was not afraid of the threat and said, "Basically I never had any idea of killing any Xiongnu people. Moreover I am not a relative of Zhang Sheng. Why do I have to be punished for a crime committed by him?" Seeing that the threat could not succeed in bringing him the result he wanted, the former Han government officer again spoke to Su Wu, "After my surrender to the Xiongnu the King treated me like his own brother. He let me be one of their government officers and gave me a lot of cattle and sheep and money. If you surrender you will be treated the same way and will live this kind of life. If you do not surrender you will be executed." Hearing this Su Wu angrily scolded him, "Not only have you betrayed your own country and become a high-ranking officer of the enemy country, but you also want me to imitate you? If a Han envoy were executed by another country the Han Government would seek revenge. If I were killed by the Xiongnu they would suffer a major disaster!"

❸   Hearing this reply the Xiongnu King wanted Su Wu to surrender all the more. He locked him up in jail and did not give him food and water. It snowed and Su Wu kept himself alive by drinking the melted snow and by eating the fur on the scepter. After several days the Xiongnu people discovered that Su Wu had not died yet. They were very surprised and thought that he was a god. The Xiongnu King dispatched Su Wu all by himself to a far away place called Bei Hai, the North Sea. (In modern time this is the Baikal Lake in Siberia.) He told him to raise sheep and Su Wu was ordered to wait for the sheep to bear lambs before he could return. In actual fact he just wanted to keep Su Wu in captivity.

❹

Sū Wǔ zài hánlěng de Běihǎi jiānkǔ de shēnghuó. Tā
苏 武 在 寒冷 的 北海 艰苦 地 生活。 他

yīzhí dài zhe dàibiǎo Hàn cháo de jiézhàng. Jiézhàng shang
一直 带 着 代表 汉 朝 的 节杖。 节杖 上

de pímáo quán dōu tuōluò le, Sū Wǔ háishi bù kěn
的 皮毛 全 都 脱落 了, 苏 武 还是 不 肯

tóuxiáng. Xiōngnúwáng yě bù ràng Sū Wǔ huí guó, yòu pài
投降。 匈奴王 也 不 让 苏 武 回国, 又 派

Sū Wǔ de péngyou Lǐ Líng lái quàn tā. Lǐ Líng shì Hàn
苏 武 的 朋友 李 陵 来 劝 他。 李 陵 是 汉

cháo rén, tóuxiáng le Xiōngnú. Lǐ Líng shuō: "Nǐ líkāi
朝 人, 投降 了 匈奴。 李 陵 说:"你 离开

Hàn cháo nàme jiǔ, Hàn cháo yǐjing fāshēng le hěn dà de
汉 朝 那么 久, 汉 朝 已经 发生 了 很 大 的

biànhuà. Nǐ de qīzi
变化。 你 的 妻子

yǐjing jià le biéren, nǐ
已经 嫁 了 别人, 你

de mǔqīn hé xiōngdi dōu
的 母亲 和 兄弟 都

sǐ le, jiārén yě shīqù
死 了, 家人 也 失去

le xiāoxi. Hàn cháo huángdì
了 消息。 汉 朝 皇帝

yǐjing lǎo le, méiyǒu
已经 老 了, 没有

《牧羊記 望鄉》
黃小午飾蘇武 石小梅飾李陵

Su Wu in drama

27

guǎn hǎo guójiā de nénglì nǐ bù tóuxiáng hái néng wèi shéi
管 好 国 家 的 能 力，你 不 投 降 还 能 为 谁

jìnzhōng ne Sū Wǔ huídá shuō Wǒ néng yǒu zhèyàng de
尽 忠 呢？"苏 武 回 答 说："我 能 有 这 样 的

dìwèi quán kào huángdì de tíbá Dàchén duì huángdì
地 位，全 靠 皇 帝 的 提 拔[6]。大 臣 对 皇 帝

zhōngxīn jiù xiàng érzi duì fùqīn xiàoshùn yīyàng Wǒ
忠 心，就 像 儿 子 对 父 亲 孝 顺 一 样。 我

nìngyuàn sǐ yě bù huì tóuxiáng
宁 愿 死，也 不 会 投 降。"

❺　　　Yòu guò le hǎo duō nián Hàn cháo zài pài shǐzhě qù
　　　又 过 了 好 多 年，汉 朝 再 派 使 者 去

Xiōngnú Tā yǔ Sū Wǔ de tóngbàn jiànmiàn cái zhīdao Sū
匈 奴。他 与 苏 武 的 同 伴 见 面，才 知 道 苏

Wǔ hái méi sǐ Hàn cháo de shǐzhě jiù duì Xiōngnúwáng
武 还 没 死。 汉 朝 的 使 者 就 对 匈 奴 王

shuō Wǒ men de huángdì zài sēnlín zhōng dǎliè shè zhòng
说："我 们 的 皇 帝 在 森 林 中 打 猎，射 中

le yī zhī dàyàn Zhè zhī dàyàn jiǎo shang yǒu yī zhāng
了 一 只 大 雁。 这 只 大 雁 脚 上 有 一 张

zhǐ xiě zhe Sū Wǔ hái méi sǐ de xiāoxi Qǐng dàiwáng bǎ
纸，写 着 苏 武 还 没 死 的 消 息。 请 大 王 把

Sū Wǔ fàng huí Hàn cháo Xiōngnúwáng hěn chījīng zhǐhǎo xiàng
苏 武 放 回 汉 朝。"匈 奴 王 很 吃 惊，只 好 向

Hàn cháo shǐzhě dàoqiàn chéngrèn Sū Wǔ hái huó zhe dāying
汉 朝 使 者 道 歉，承 认 苏 武 还 活 着，答 应

bǎ Sū Wǔ fàng huí Hàn cháo Zhè shí Sū Wǔ yǐjing zài
把 苏 武 放 回 汉 朝，这 时，苏 武 已 经 在

Xiōngnú jiānkǔ de shēnghuó le shí jiǔ nián
匈 奴 艰 苦 地 生 活 了 十 九 年。

GLOSSARY

6 提拔 promote

28

Translation

❹   Su Wu lived a very hard life in bitterly cold Beihai, the North Sea. He always carried the scepter that represented the Han Government. The fur on the scepter had all fallen off and Su Wu still refused to surrender. But, the Xiongnu King would not let him go back to his own country . Then he sent Li Ling, a friend of Su Wu, to try to convince him to surrender. Li Ling was a Han who had surrendered to the Xiongnu. He said to Su Wu, "The Han Government which you left a long time ago has undergone great changes. Your wife has remarried another person. Your mother and brothers have all died. No one has any news regarding what has happened to the rest of your family members. The Han Emperor has become very old and does not have the ability to govern the country well. If you do not surrender to the Xiongnu who else are you going to be loyal to?" Su Wu replied, "The reason why I hold a status as honorable as this one is all because of the grace of the Emperor's promotion. The loyalty of a high-ranking government officer to his Emperor is like the filial piety of a son towards his father. I would rather die than surrender."

❺   After many years the Han Government sent another diplomat to the Xiongnu. Only when he met Su Wu's companions did he know that Su Wu had not yet died. This Han diplomat said to the King of Xiongnu, "Our Emperor was hunting in the forest. He shot down a big wild goose, on the leg of which a piece of paper was attached. A message was written on that paper saying that Su Wu had not died yet. Your Highness! Please release him so that he can go home." The Xiongnu King was very shocked and could only apologize to the Han diplomat. He admitted that Su Wu was still alive and promised to let Su Wu return home to the State of Han. Up to that point in time Su Wu had already lived a very bitter life in the Xiongnu territories for 19 years.

❻

Sū Wǔ hé tóngbàn chūshǐ Xiōngnú shí háishi hēi
苏 武 和 同伴 出使 匈奴 时 还是 黑

tóufa de zhōngnián rén dàn dāng tāmen jǔ zhe guāngtūtū de
头发 的 中年人，但 当 他们 举 着 光秃秃 的

jiézhàng huí dào zìjǐ de guójiā shí tóufa húzi dōu
节杖 回 到 自己 的 国家 时 ， 头发 胡子 都

yǐjing biàn de cāngbái Huí dào Hàn cháo yǐhòu tāmen chéng
已经 变 得 苍白 。 回 到 汉朝 以后 ， 他们 成

le guójiā zhòngyào de guānyuán
了 国家 重要 的 官员 。

Translation

❻ When Su Wu and his companions were sent to the Xiongnu as diplomats, they were dark-haired middle-aged people. On their return, the scepter they held high up in the air was bare and bald without any fur anymore and their hair and beards had become all white. After their return to the Han Government they became very important government officers.

The Place for Raising Sheep

The place where Su Wu raised and tended his sheep was called Beihai, which is the Baikal Lake in Siberia in modern times. In the Xihan Dynasty (202 B.C. to 8 A.D.) Beihai was within the Xiongnu boundaries and under their control. Before the Qing Dynasty (1636 to 1911), the Baikal Lake had always been the nomadic area of the tribes in northern China. When the Czar in Russia expanded to the East, the Baikal Lake came under Russian control.

The meaning of Baikal is "a natural sea". It was formed approximately 250 million years ago. It is one of the oldest lakes and at the same time it is the biggest and deepest fresh water lake in the world. It contains one fifth of all the fresh water on earth. Its capacity is equal to the total water capacity of the Five Great Lakes of North America. The Baikal Lake, shaped like an ecliptic moon, is long, narrow and looped-shaped. Therefore it is also called the "Moon Lake". The lake water is crystal clear. Within the lake abundant and various species of living organisms can be found. There is the viviparous Baikal Lake fish and the Coregonus autumnali and over one thousand other unique species, which cannot be found elsewhere. The weather of the Baikal Lake region is suitable for living and its scenery is like that in a painting. There are many natural and archeological sites and many extraordinary and unique living species that attract a lot of tourists. It has been listed as a natural heritage site of the world by the United Nations Educational, Scientific and Cultural Organization (UNESCO).

GAMES FOR FUN

Beihai is in the cold area of modern day Siberia. Please circle the terms related to cold weather: 酷寒、冷静、冷气、冷清、寒流、冰冻

Bān Chāo zhì shā Xiōngnú shǐzhě

班超智杀匈奴使者

With a Clever Strategic Plan Ban Chao Killed All the Xiongnu Diplomats

Pre-reading Questions

1. Can you make a guess as to the average number of members in a diplomatic mission in ancient China?

2. The Emperors in ancient China sent military soldiers as diplomats. Was it possible that they were expected to fight if battles broke out? What is your interpretation of this kind of arrangement?

❶

Bān Chāo shì Hàn cháo zhùmíng de wàijiāo jiā hé dà
班 超 是 汉 朝 著名 的 外交 家 和 大

jiāngjūn　　Tā běnlái shì gè dúshū rén dànshì yǒu yī
将军。 他 本来 是 个 读书 人，但是 有 一

tiān tā juéde zuò jūnrén gèng yǒu yìsi yúshì jiārù
天 他 觉得 做 军人 更 有 意思，于是 加入

jūnduì　　Hàn cháo běnlái kāituò[1] le Sīchóu zhī lù kěyǐ
军队。 汉 朝 本来 开拓[1] 了 丝绸之路，可以

tōng dào Xīyù de guójiā hòulái yīnwèi nèibù
通 到 西域 的 国家，后来 因为 内部

dǎzhàng Sīchóu zhī lù yòu bù tōng le Běifāng de Xiōngnú[2]
打仗，丝绸之路 又 不 通 了。北方 的 匈奴[2]

是 一 个 游牧 民族，军事 力量 很 强，这
时候 经常 骚扰[3] 汉朝。于是 汉朝 派 班超
做 使者，带 着 三 十 六 个 人 到 西域，要
说服 西域 的 国家 跟 汉朝 结交，一起 对抗
匈奴。

❷ 班超 首先 到 了 西域 的 一 个
国家，叫做 鄯善。起初，鄯善 国王 待 他们
很 好，但 不久 就 不 理 他们 了。班超 感到
事情 不 平常，就 对 一起 来 的 人 说："你们
有 没有 发现 鄯善 国王 态度 变 了？一定

Ban Chao was the Chinese diplomat who visited many countries of Xiyu,
which is the location of modern Xinjiang, the Middle East and Western Asia

<table>
<tr><td>shì</td><td>Xiōngnú</td><td>yě</td><td>pài</td><td>le</td><td>rén</td><td>lái</td><td>suǒyǐ</td><td>tā</td><td>biàn</td><td>bù</td><td>yuànyì</td></tr>
</table>

是 匈奴 也 派 了 人 来，所以 他 便 不 愿意

jiējìn wǒmen

接近 我们 。 ”

GLOSSARY

1 开拓　develop
2 匈奴　the Huns
3 骚扰　harass

Translation

❶　Ban Chao was a famous diplomat and a grand general during the Han Dynasty. Originally he was a scholar. But one day he felt that it would be more meaningful to be a soldier. Then he joined the army. In the Han Dynasty, the Silk Road (Sichouzhilu) had already been developed and people could travel all the way to the countries in Xiyu. Later on the Silk Road was blocked because of wars among the Xiongnu. The Xiongnu was a northern nomadic tribe, which was very strong militarily. During that period of time it frequently harassed the Han Dynasty, the government of which then sent Ban Chao to lead a mission of 36 people to Xiyu with the purpose of convincing the countries of Xiyu to form an alliance with China to defend themselves against the Xiongnu.

❷　Ban Chao reached Shanshan, the first Xiyu country. At first the King of Shanshan treated them very well. But not very long after that he neglected them and did not care to look after them. Ban Chao felt that something extraordinary was happening. He talked to his followers, "Have you found that the attitude of the King of Shanshan has changed? The Xiongnu must have sent their people here too. That is why the Shanshan King is not willing to associate with us."

❸ 为了查明真相，班超故意问一
个鄯善国的官员："我知道匈奴的使者
来了好几天了，不知道现在住在
哪里？"这个官员听了，害怕起来，就把
匈奴使者的情况告诉班超。原来匈奴的
人，比班超他们多几倍。

❹ 班超为了不让消息泄露[4]，把鄯善国
的官员关起来，然后把跟他来的三十六
个人叫来，一起喝酒。当大家喝得非常
痛快的时候，班超对他们说："大家这次
来西域，都希望能够为国家立大功。现在

Camels were used as the major means of transportation of the Silk Route

匈奴 的 使者 来 了，鄯善 国王 立即 对 我们
很 冷淡。 如果 国王 把 我们 抓 起来，送 给
匈奴 的 使者，那 我们 不 是 白白 成 了 狼 的
食物！ 大家 有 什么 方法 解决 呢？"

❺ 大家 听 了，一起 说："我们 现在 很
危险，在 这个 生 死 关头。 我们 都 听 你
的 话，请 你 出 主意 吧！" 班 超 很 明确 地
说："不 进 老虎 的 山洞，怎么 能够 得 到 小
老虎？ 眼前 只有 一 个 办法，今天 晚上 我们
一起 用 火 进攻 匈奴 的 使者，他们 不 知 我们
有 多少 人，一定 感到 害怕，我们 就 借 这个
机会 消灭 他们。 消灭 了 匈奴 使者，鄯善 国王
就 愿意 和 我们 和好。 只有 这样，我们 才 可以
逃 过 大难，建立 大 功。"大家 都 说："好"。

GLOSSARY

4 泄露　leak

Translation

❸   In order to find out the real situation Ban Chao purposely asked a Shanshan government officer. He said, "I know that the Xiongnu diplomats have been here for quite a few days now. I do not know where they are staying, do you?" Hearing this that government officer was scared and told Ban Chao the whereabouts of the Xiongnu diplomats. Actually, the people sent by the Xiongnu numbered several times more than Ban Chao and his followers.

❹   In order not to leak out this bad news Ban Chao locked up that government officer. Then he summoned all the 36 followers to gather for a drinking party. When everyone was heartily enjoying their wine Ban Chao said to them, "In this Xiyu diplomatic mission we all hope to establish some major achievements for our country. But now that the Xiongnu diplomats have arrived, the Shanshan King has immediately cooled down his association with us. If he captures us and sends us to the Xiongnu diplomats then we would be like the food thrown to the wolves. Our lives would be wasted for nothing. Do you people have any solution?"

❺   Hearing this all his followers said to Ban Chao together, "We are now in great danger. At this critical moment of life and death we will all listen to you. Please suggest an idea!" Very decisively Ban Chao said, "Without entering the tiger's den how can we obtain the little tiger cubs? Right before our eyes there is only one solution. Tonight as a group we will use fire to attack the Xiongnu diplomats. Since they do not know how many of us there are they must feel scared. We will make use of this opportunity to eliminate them. After their elimination the Shanshan King will be willing to make peace with us. This is our only way to escape from a major disaster and to establish a major achievement." Everyone said, "Good idea!"

❻ Dào le wǎnshang Bān Chāo tāmen jiù jìngjìng qù dào
到 了 晚上, 班 超 他们 就 静静 去 到

Xiōngnú shǐzhě zhù de dìfang Bān Chāo fēnfù shí gè
匈奴 使者 住 的 地方。 班 超 吩咐 十 个

rén ná zhe jūngǔ duǒ zài wū hòu yī jiàn dà huǒ shāo
人 拿 着 军鼓, 躲 在 屋 后, 一 见 大 火 烧

qǐlai lìkè dǎ gǔ dà shēng hǎnjiào Qítā rén jiù
起来, 立刻 打 鼓, 大 声 喊叫。 其他 人 就

dài shang wǔqì máifú zài dà mén liǎng páng Nà tiān
带 上 武器, 埋伏[5] 在 大 门 两旁。 那 天

wǎnshang zhènghǎo guā dàfēng Bān Chāo zài shàng fēng de dìfang diǎn
晚上 正好 刮 大风, 班 超 在 上 风 的 地方 点

huǒ qiánhòu zuǒyòu de rén yīqǐ dǎgǔ hūhǎn Xiōngnú
火, 前后 左右 的 人 一起 打鼓 呼喊。 匈奴

rén jiàndào huǒguāng xióngxióng dōu jīnghuāng luàn zǒu Zuìhòu Bān
人 见到 火光 熊熊, 都 惊慌[6] 乱 走。 最后, 班

Chāo shùnlì shā sǐ suǒyǒu Xiōngnú rén bìngqiě bǎ Xiōngnú
超 顺利 杀 死 所有 匈奴 人, 并且 把 匈奴

shǐzhě de tóu ná gěi Shànshàn guówáng kàn Shànshàn quán guó
使者 的 头 拿 给 鄯善 国王 看。 鄯善 全 国

zhèndòng cóngcǐ gēn Hàn cháo yīqǐ duìfu Xiōngnú
震动, 从此 跟 汉朝 一起 对付 匈奴。

Fighting against the Xiongnu people

❼

後來 班 超 代表 中國 出使 西域 很
多 次，他 又 機智 又 勇敢，立 下 不 少 大
功。他 年老 的 時候，請求 回到 中國，他
跟 皇帝 說："我 不 敢 要求 回到 首都，只要
能 進入 中國 境，就 很 滿足 了。"但是 他
從 西域 回來，還 沒有 進入 中國 的 關口，就
去世 了。

GLOSSARY

5 埋伏 ambush　　　6 惊慌 scared

Translation

❻　　When night came Ban Chao and his followers quietly went to where the Xiongnu stayed. He told ten people, equipped with military drums, to hide around the house. When they saw a fire starting to burn they were to immediately beat the drums and shout loudly. The rest of them would carry their weapons and hide beside the two sides of the main gate. Luckily for them strong winds were blowing that night. Ban Chao started the fire in the up wind area. From all four directions, the front, the back, the left and the right, people in unison beat the drums and shouted in a loud voice. Seeing the bright fire the Xiongnu people were scared and tried to escape wildly in all directions. Ban Chao and his followers easily killed all the Xiongnu diplomats. He also brought the Shanshan King to see the Xiongnu diplomats' heads. The whole Shanshan country was shocked. From then on Shanshan formed an alliance with the Han Dynasty to deal with the Xiongnu.

⑦   Later on Ban Chao, representing China as a diplomat, visited Xiyu many times. He was both brave and clever and accomplished a lot of major achievements. When he became old he requested to return to China. He said to the Emperor, "I dare not ask to be allowed to return to the capital. I would be very satisfied if I could enter the Chinese territories." But on his way back from Xiyu he died before he could enter the Chinese customs office.

Exchanges between China and the West

When Ban Chao was sent to Xiyu as a Han diplomat he traveled on the Silk Road which began at Han capital cities: It began at Chang An (called Xi'an), the capital of the Xihan Dynasty. And it began at Luo Yang, the capital of the Donghan Dynasty. It passed through Gan Su, Lan Zhou, and the He Xi Corridor(called Jiu Quan and Dun Huang now). It exited through Yu Men Guan, or Yang Guan, reaching Luo Bu Bo and then passed through middle Asia, Persia (called Iran now), and Arabia, before going to the Ancient Roman Empire which traded with many countries in Europe and Northern Africa. As a result of this traffic network the multilateral exchanges among China, Eurasia, and Africa increased quickly.

In trade Chinese products like silk fabrics, porcelain wares, gold, silver and iron utensils were continuously exported to Eurasia. On top of these products, the ancient printing technology of China and paper products spread westward through the Silk Road. Herbs, gems and new species of plants were imported into China. Religions like Buddhism, Manicheism, Nestorianism and Christianity came to China through the Silk Road too. The Silk Road facilitated the exchanges between China and the West. Among the products exported to the west, silk products had the biggest influence and this was why a German scholar in the 19th century named this route as the Silk Road.

Zhūgě Liàng cǎo chuán jiè jiàn

诸葛亮草船借箭

Zhuge Liang "Makes" Arrows Using Boats Stuffed with Straw

With a feather-fan in his hand the confidence of Zhuge Liang as a wise man was vividly portrayed

Pre-reading Questions

1. Human-look-alike straw bundles were able to "borrow" things from other people. Do you want to know what they "borrowed"?

2. If you were a general fighting a battle in a very thick fog, would you issue an order to attack or retreat?

---

❶
Zhūgě Liàng shì Sānguó shídài gōngyuán
诸葛 亮 是 三国 时代（ 公元 184 — 280

nián yī gè hěn yǒu jìmóu de rén Zhōu Yú shífēn dùjì¹
年）一 个 很 有 计谋 的 人，周 瑜 十分 妒忌¹

tā Yǒu yī cì Zhūgě Liàng yào hé Zhōu Yú yīqǐ qù
他。 有 一 次， 诸葛 亮 要 和 周 瑜 一起 去

hé Cáo Cāo zuòzhàn Zhōu Yú xiǎng jìn bànfǎ xiǎng xiànhài²
和 曹 操 作战。 周 瑜 想 尽 办法， 想 陷害²

Zhūgě Liàng Tā xiǎng ràng Zhūgě Liàng zài shí tiān nèi zào hǎo
诸葛 亮。 他 想 让 诸葛 亮 在 十 天 内 造 好

shí wàn zhī jiàn rúguǒ Zhūgě Liàng bù néng ànshí wánchéng
十 万 支 箭， 如果 诸葛 亮 不 能 按时 完成

rènwù nà jiù kěyǐ chǔfá tā le Zhōu Yú yòu jiào zuò
任务， 那 就 可以 处罚 他 了。 周 瑜 又 叫 做

41

jiàn de rén gùyì bù zhǔnbèi hǎo zào jiàn de cáiliào　Dì
箭 的 人 故意 不 准备 好 造 箭 的 材料。 第

èr tiān Zhōu Yú biàn qǐng Zhūgě Liàng lái shāngliang zào jiàn
二 天， 周 瑜 便 请 诸葛 亮 来 商量 造 箭

de shìqing Bùliào Zhūgě Liàng bùdàn dāying zào jiàn hái
的 事情。 不料 诸葛 亮 不但 答应 造 箭， 还

biǎoshì tā zhǐyào sān tiān jiù kěyǐ wánchéng rènwù Tā
表示 他 只要 三 天 就 可以 完成 任务。 他

ràng Zhōu Yú sān tiān hòu qù jiāng biān bān jiàn ránhòu biàn zǒu
让 周 瑜 三 天 后 去 江 边 搬 箭，然后 便 走

le
了。

GLOSSARY

1 妒忌　envy
2 陷害　frame

Translation

❶　During the Period of the Three Kingdoms (184 – 280 A.D.) there was an ingenious strategist called Zhuge Liang. Zhou Yu was extremely jealous of him. Once they had to partner together to fight against Cao Cao. Zhou Yu thought of each and every means to frame Zhuge Liang. He wanted Zhuge Liang to assume the mission of manufacturing 100,000 arrows within ten days. If he could not fulfill the mission then he would be penalized. Also Zhou Yu had purposely asked the arrow makers not to prepare the materials for producing arrows. The next day Zhou Yu invited Zhuge Liang over to talk about the details of making the arrows. At their meeting Zhuge Liang's response was unexpected by Zhou Yu. He not only promised to take on the arrow-making mission but he also said he only needed three days to finish the job. He asked Zhou Yu to go to the riverside to collect the arrows after three days. Then Zhuge Liang left.

❷ 周瑜 觉得 奇怪:"这么 难 的 任务,诸葛亮 怎么 那么 轻松 呢?"他 派 鲁肃 去 探听 消息。鲁肃 是 个 好人,他 为 诸葛亮 造 箭 的 事 很 担心。诸葛亮 一 见 鲁肃 便 说:"造 箭 得 请 你 帮帮 我 啊!"他 向 鲁肃 借 了 二十 条 船,船 都 用 青 布 遮 起来。还 要 用 稻草 做 成 人 的 样子,放 在 船 的 两边。每 条 船 上 要 三 十 名 士兵 和 一 千 个 草人。同时,他 请 鲁肃 不 要 向 周瑜 报告 这些 事情。鲁肃 都 答应 了。

Zhuge Liang borrowed straw to make one thousand straw men

❸ 船 都 准备 好 了。可 第 一 天,诸葛亮 没有 行动。第 二 天,还是 没有 行动。直到 第 三 天 夜 里,诸葛亮 秘密 请 鲁肃 来 到

jiāng biān　bìngqiě　gàosu　Lǔ Sù　yào qù qǔ jiàn　Lǔ Sù
江 边 ，并且 告诉 鲁 肃 要 去 取 箭 。 鲁 肃

juéde　hěn　qíguài　Qù　nǎli　qǔ jiàn　a　Zhūgě Liàng
觉得 很 奇怪 ：" 去 哪里 取 箭 啊 ？ " 诸葛 亮

huídá　Děng　yīxià　jiù　zhīdao　le
回答 ：" 等 一下 就 知道 了 。 "

Translation

❷　　Zhou Yu felt very strange and said to himself, "How can Zhuge Liang assume a duty as difficult as this so easily?" He sent Lu Su to find out the latest news on what was happening. Lu Su was a nice person and he was very worried for Zhuge Liang about his arrow-making mission. When Zhuge Liang saw Lu Su he said to him immediately, "Please help me in this arrow-making matter." He borrowed 20 boats from Lu Su. Each boat was covered with green cloth. Also human-shaped bundles were made from straw and these were placed on both sides of each boat. Every boat was equipped with 30 soldiers and one thousand "straw men". At the same time as making these requests Zhuge Liang also asked Lu Su not to report them to Zhou Yu. Lu Su promised to fulfill all the requests that Zhuge Liang had made.

❸　　All the boats were prepared as ordered. But on the first day Zhuge Liang did not take any action. On the second day he did not do anything either. Only until nightfall of the third day did Zhuge Liang secretly invite Lu Su to come to the riverside and tell him that they were going to go and collect arrows. Lu Su felt that Zhuge Liang was acting strange and asked him, "Where are we going to collect arrows?" Zhuge Liang replied, "Wait for a little while and then you will know."

❹ 这时候江上雾很大，看不到远的地方。诸葛亮派人将二十条船用绳子连在一起，朝北岸曹操军队那儿开去。天还没亮，船队就

The story of Zhuge Liang has its origin from the novel, *Romances of the Three Kingdoms*

接近北岸了。诸葛亮命令将船队横排成一列。然后又叫士兵一边打鼓，一边大声叫。鲁肃十分害怕，说："如果曹操的军队出来，怎么办啊？"诸葛亮笑着说："放心吧！雾那么大，曹操的军队不会出来的。我们继续喝酒吧，天亮了就回去。"曹操听到鼓声和叫声，立即出来看。他见雾那么大，担心是个圈套³，果然没有派军队出来攻打。他只是命令一万个士兵向江中射箭，阻止敌人靠岸。一时间，箭像下雨一样，射在船

上 的 草人 上。 过 了 一阵，诸葛 亮 又 命令

船队 调转 方向，用 另 一 面 去 受 箭，并 让

士兵 继续 打鼓 叫喊。 曹 操 的 士兵 仍然

拼命 向 江 中 射箭。 等 到 太阳 出来 的

时候，船 上 的 草人 上 已经 插 满 了 箭。 这

时候，诸 葛 亮 才 下令 船 队 回去。 他 还

让 士兵 一齐 大 叫："谢谢 你 的 箭！"曹 操

知道 上当 了，可惜 船 队 已经 走 远 了，要

追 也 追 不 上 了。

❺　　诸 葛 亮 的 船 回来 的

时候，周 瑜 派 来 的 士兵

正好 来 搬 箭。 每 条 船

大约 五、六 千 支 箭，总共

Boats are stuffed with 100,000
arrows

便 有 十 万 支 箭。 原来，诸 葛 亮 懂得 天文

知识，三 天 前 便 知道 会 有 大 雾 了。

GLOSSARY

3 圈套　trap

Translation

❹   At that time the river was covered with a very thick fog. Visibility was limited and one could not see very far. Zhuge Liang sent people to use ropes to link up the 20 boats and sent the linked-up fleet towards the northern shore where the Cao army was stationed. Before dawn the fleet approached the northern shore. Zhuge Liang ordered the men to line up the boats as one line (longitudinally bow-to-stern-wise). Then he ordered the soldiers to beat the drums and to shout loudly at the same time. Lu Su was very afraid and said, "If the Cao army comes out what are we going to do?" Zhuge Liang laughed and said to him, "Relax and don't worry! In this thick fog the Cao army will not come out. Let's continue drinking our wine. When the day brightens up we can go back." When Cao Cao heard the drums and the shouting he immediately came out to take a look. He saw the thick fog and worried that it was a trap. As expected by Zhuge Liang, Cao Cao did not send his army out to attack. He only ordered 10,000 soldiers to shoot arrows towards the middle of the river in order to stop the enemy from approaching the shore. Immediately, arrows fell down like rain into the straw men. After a little while Zhuge Liang ordered the fleet to change to the opposite direction, using the other side to collect arrows. He let the soldiers continue beating the drums and shouting. The soldiers of Cao's army continued to shoot arrows towards the middle of the river as if it were a matter of life or death. When the sun came out the straw people on the boats were full of arrows. It was only until that moment that Zhuge Liang ordered the fleet to return home. He also let the soldiers shout simultaneously, "Thank you for your arrows." Cao Cao then knew that he had been fooled by a setup. But the fleet was long gone and it was too late to be able to catch up to the enemy.

❺   When Zhuge Liang's fleet returned it was just in time for Zhou Yu's soldiers to come to collect the arrows. Each boat had about five to six thousand arrows. Altogether there were about 100,000 arrows. The reason why this clever strategy worked was that Zhuge Liang had a very good knowledge of astronomy. Three days before he knew there would be a thick fog.

Zhuge Liang in Novels, Movies and Comics

In the novel *Romance of the Three Kingdoms*, Zhuge Liang is an intelligent strategist with a bagful of clever tricks. He plans his policies in such detail that all changes, anticipated or unexpected, are taken care of. He has outstanding abilities to govern the country and to command the army. Moreover he never uses his high status to make personal gain. He is extremely loyal to Liu Bei and the State of Shu.

Because of the popularity of *Romance of the Three Kingdoms*, themes and episodes were extracted from it and then they were converted into opera performances, some of the most well-known are "Kongchengji, the Deceptive Strategy of an Empty Castle", "Qunyinghui, the Gathering of Super Heroes" and "Jiedongfeng, Borrowing the East Blowing Wind". In these opera performances basing on the *Romance of the Three Kingdoms* the character of Zhuge Liang is played by an actor specializing in acting in an old male role. The image created is an older gentleman, holding a feather fan in his right hand, and wearing a headscarf tied with a matching green silk ribbon. In actual fact, Zhuge Liang was not even 30 in the year of the Battle of Chibi in which he decisively defeated Cao Cao. In the opera performances Zhuge Liang has been molded to appear as a middle-aged character because they want to accentuate his special attributes of calm, stability and his outstanding brilliance in strategic planning. In modern TV dramas and movies Zhuge Liang is also portrayed as a middle-aged man, holding a feather fan in his right hand with the stage appearance of a sage. In games and comics Zhuge Liang appears as a comparatively younger person with a moustache and a goatee, holding a feather fan in his right hand. Although this is the same Zhuge Liang as portrayed in the novel and the operas, yet he looks younger and more handsome.

In *Romance of the Three Kingdoms*, during the time of the Battle of Chibi when Zhou Yu was cooperating with as well as competing with Zhuge Liang in tricking each other, Zhou Yu was in actual fact older than Zhuge Liang. According to historical records he was a man famous for being handsome. Therefore in opera he appears with a young and handsome face all the time. According to historical records Zhou Yu was the real hero in the Battle of Chibi and he was also very good in music.

GAMES FOR FUN

Guess who is Zhuge Liang in this film poster.

Zhuge Liang

Zhào Yún

赵云 ——

bǎiwàn jūn zhōng jiù shàozhǔ

百万军中救少主

Zhao Yun – Rescues His Master's Son from the Army of One Million Soldiers

Pre-reading Questions

1. Do you want to learn more about this hero of ancient China who took a great risk of dying in order to carry out an act of rescue for the son of another person?

2. What would be your immediate reaction when you are misunderstood?

❶
Zài Sānguó zhànzhēng li Zhào Yún bèi chēng wéi cháng shèng
在 三 国 战 争 里，赵 云 被 称 为 长 胜
jiāngjūn
将军。

❷
Tā hěn zǎo jiù gēnsuí
他 很 早 就 跟随

Liú Bèi dāngshí Liú Bèi
刘 备，当时 刘 备
bīnglì bù qiáng zhǐyǒu jǐ
兵 力 不 强，只有 几
qiān shìbīng méiyǒu zìjǐ
千 士兵，没有 自己
de tǔdì
的 土地。

Zhao Yun's image in on-line games

❸ 有一次，他带着军队去投靠[1]其他人，赵云负责保护刘备的夫人和儿子。因为有很多老百姓跟着刘备，所以他们每天只可以走十几里，这时已快冬天，天气寒冷，山头到处听到老百姓的哭声。大家走得很疲倦，晚上在山边休息。

❹ 没想到半夜里，敌人突然出现。在这危急[2]时候，刘备和将士分别作战，结果他和赵云，以及很多将士失散了，只有很少人跟他一起逃出敌人的包围。他们刚刚冲出包围，一个受伤的将士跑来报告："赵云投降去了！"刘备大吃一惊，说："赵云不会背叛我。"但是那个将士说他是亲眼看见的。急躁的张飞在旁边听见，生气

de shuō Wǒ qù zhǎo Zhào Yún rúguǒ pèngjian le wǒ yī
地 说:"我 去 找 赵 云,如果 碰 见 了,我 一

qiāng cì sǐ tā Liú Bèi quàn tā Bù yào chōngdòng Zhào
枪 刺 死 他。"刘 备 劝 他:"不 要 冲 动³,赵

Yún zài wǒ zuì kùnnan de shíhou gēncóng wǒ tā bù huì
云 在 我 最 困 难 的 时候 跟 从 我,他 不 会

wèile fùguì ér dòngyáo de Rúguǒ tā dào dírén nà
为了 富贵 而 动摇 的。如果 他 到 敌人 那

biān yīdìng yǒu yuányīn
边,一定 有 原因。"

GLOSSARY

1 投靠 seek shelter
2 危急 emergency
3 冲动 act on impulse

Portrait of Liu Bei(left) and Zhang Fei(right)

Translation

❶   In the battles of the Three Kingdoms, Zhao Yun was called the forever-invincible general.

❷   At an early age he had started to follow Liu Bei, who at that time was not very strong militarily. He only had a few thousand soldiers then and did not have his own territories. Once, he even had to lead his army to go to another leader to seek shelter.

❸   Zhao Yun was responsible for the protection of Lady Liu Bei (Gan) and her son. Because there were a lot of common people following Liu Bei therefore they could only advance about ten miles each day. It was nearly wintertime and the weather was cold. Everywhere on the mountain one could hear people crying. Everyone was very tired from all the walking. At night people rested by the side of the mountain.

❹   No one could have imagined that at midnight the enemy would suddenly appear. At this moment of emergency, Liu Bei and his generals and soldiers were fighting different groups of the enemy and, as a result, he and Zhao Yun and many other generals and soldiers were completely separated from each other, losing contact altogether. Only a few people followed Liu Bei to escape from the surrounding enemy. Just as they charged out from the besieging soldiers, an injured soldier came to report to Liu Bei saying, "Zhao Yun has surrendered." Greatly shocked Liu Bei said, "Zhao Yun would not betray me." But the injured soldier said he saw it with his own eyes. When the impatient Zhang Fei, who was standing at his side, heard this he said angrily, "I shall go and look for Zhao Yun. If I meet up with him I will use my spear to kill him in one single strike." Liu Bei tried to calm Zhang Fei down and advised him, "Do not act on impulse. Zhao Yun came to follow me when I was at my most difficult time. His loyalty to me would not waver with a promise of wealth and social esteem from the other side. If he went over to the side of the enemy there must be a reason."

❺ 另一方面，自从半夜里突然出现敌人，赵云来回杀敌，一直到天亮。他一边作战一边前进，忽然发现不见了刘备、夫人和少主。他想："我负责夫人和少主，现在不见了，我怎么办呢？即使和敌人拼命，我也要把夫人和少主抢回来。"他看看左右，身边只有三四十人。赵云带领他们回去到处寻找。

❻ 路边很多老百姓受伤倒下，或者丢下儿女。赵云到处找，拼命杀死敌人，后来自己的人也一个不剩了。

❼ 终于他见到夫人抱着少主，坐在没有水的井旁不断地哭。赵云急忙说："请快上马，我走路，保护你出去。"夫人说："将军打仗，怎么能不骑马，你赶快抱走少主，不要理

我。可怜我的丈夫年纪大了，只有这个儿子，只要儿子能生存，我死也无所谓。"赵云再三催夫人上马，她怎么也不上。眼看敌人快要来到，赵云高声喝："你不走，怎么办呢？"突然夫人丢下儿子，自己跳到井里。赵云为了防止敌人抢去尸体，他推倒土墙，盖好枯井。接着他解开铁甲，将少主放在怀里，拿枪上马，直冲出去。

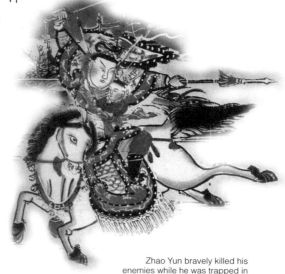

Zhao Yun bravely killed his enemies while he was trapped in the army of a million soldiers

Translation

❺   On the other side of the mountain, since the appearance of the enemy at midnight, Zhao Yun had been fighting and killing them here and there till dawn in order to advance. All of a sudden he discovered the disappearance of Liu Bei and his family, Lady Gan and her son. He thought to himself, "I am responsible for the safety of Lady Gan and my young master. Now they have disappeared. What am I going to do? Even if I have to fight the enemy until death I have to get them back." He looked left and right and saw only 30 to 40 followers by his side. He led them everywhere to conduct his search.

❻   By the roadside a lot of common people had fallen with injuries. And some of them had abandoned their children. Zhao Yun searched everywhere, killing the enemy as it was a matter of life or death. Finally, all of his own people were gone. Not a single one was left behind.

❼   Finally, he saw Lady Gan holding his young master to her bosom and sitting beside a waterless well, crying non-stop. Hurriedly Zhao Yun said, "Please quickly mount my horse. I'll walk to protect you all the way to safety." Lady Gan said, "How can a general fight a battle without the rapid mobility of riding a horse? Please quickly take your young master and run. You do not need to take care of me. My poor husband is quite old. This is his only son. If my death can ensure the baby's survival I do not mind to die." Repeatedly Zhao Yun urged Lady Gan to get on the horse. She kept on refusing. They both could see that the enemy was going to catch up to them soon. Zhao Yun shouted in a loud voice, "If you refuse to go what are we going to do?" All of a sudden Lady Gan left her son on the ground and jumped into the well. To prevent the enemy from robbing her body and taking it away he pushed and collapsed a dirt wall to cover up the dry well. Then he untied his iron armor and put his young master inside. He took up his spear and mounted his horse and charged his way out.

❽ 这时早有敌人赶上来，赵云刚刚冲出包围，又被另一支敌人拦住。他奋力[4]冲杀，见人就刺。

❾ 敌人的主帅远远看见赵云，问："这个勇猛像老虎的人是谁？大家不要放箭，我要活捉他！"赵云使尽全身力气，保护少主，砍倒两面大旗，杀死敌人大将五十人，衣服全染了鲜血，一直杀出重围，终于脱险。

❿ 见到刘备，他急忙下马，跪下来说："我实在对不起你，就是我死一万次，也无法补救。夫人受了重伤，不肯上马，跳井死了。我只好把少主抱在怀里，冲出包围。少主刚才还在哭，现在已听不见声音，恐怕也活不成了。"说着解开衣甲一看，原来少主

呼呼大睡。赵云高兴地把少主递给刘
备。刘备接过儿子，一下子把他扔在
地上，流着泪说："为你这孩子，几乎叫
我失去了一个大将。"赵云连忙把少主
抱起来，感动地说："你对我的恩惠⁵，我
永远不会忘记。"

GLOSSARY

4 奋力　try one's very best to do something
5 恩惠　favor

Translation

❽　At this moment a lot of enemy soldiers rushed over. Just emerging from a group of the besieging enemy, Zhao Yun was blocked by another group of the enemy. He furiously charged and killed, piercing anyone in sight with his spear.

❾　From afar the chief general of the enemy saw Zhao Yun and asked, "Who is this man as brave as a tiger? Don't shoot him down with arrows. I want to capture him alive!" Zhao Yun used the strength of his whole body to protect his young master. Using a knife he hacked down two big military flags of the enemy and killed 50 of their generals. His clothes were all covered with fresh blood. He charged his way out from the rings of the surrounding enemy and escaped from the dangerous situation.

❿　When he saw Liu Bei he hurriedly dismounted from his horse and knelt down and said, "Sir! I am really sorry! Even dying ten thousand times cannot compensate for my fault. The severely injured Lady Gan kept on refusing to mount the horse to escape. She then jumped into the well and killed herself. I could only carry my young master in my bosom and charge my way out of the surrounding enemy. I heard him crying a little while ago and now I cannot hear any sound. I am afraid he might not be alive." After saying this he untied his armor and took a look and saw that the snoring baby was sleeping soundly. He was very happy and handed his young master to Liu Bei, who took his son and immediately threw him on the ground and said with tears, "All because of this baby I have nearly lost a great general." Zhao Yun quickly picked up the baby and deeply moved he said emotionally to Liu Bei, "I will never forget the favor you have bestowed on me."

The Five Tiger Generals in *Romance of the Three Kingdoms*

In the novel *Romance of the Three Kingdoms*, Guan Yu, Zhang Fei, Zhao Yun, Ma Chao and Huang Zhong were very outstanding generals. Together they were called the "Five Tiger Generals".
Guan Yu was the head of the "Five Tiger Generals". His appearance looked majestic and military. He had great strength and held a long-handled giant knife, called the Green Dragon. He was awe-inspiring, intelligent and brave and had always been recognized as a model person, who would take great care to keep his promises and to uphold the principle of trustworthiness and justice. Zhang Fei used an eighteen-foot long snake spear as his weapon. He was both brave and strong. His enemies were very frightened of him. Once at Changbanpo leading a 20-member cavalry unit he scared away the army of Cao Cao. In addition he was a very cultured person, a very famous calligrapher and painter. But he was relatively hot-tempered. Zhao Yun was nearly perfect. He was gentle, not snobbish, honest and militarily and culturally accomplished. Zhao Yun saved Liu Bei's son on his own, charging his way out of the closely surrounding

enemy. He acted strong and brave. Ma Chao wore a white robe and a set of silver helmet and armor, riding a white horse. People called him the "bright and beautiful Ma Chao". In the major battle of Tongguan he led the army and decisively defeated the army of Cao. Cao Cao was so hard-pressed by Ma's army that he had to cut off his beard and abandon his robe, escaping the chase in a very embarrassing manner. Huang Zhong was a very sharp arrow shooter. He would shoot one hundred arrows and all the arrows would hit the targets. In the war against the Cao army, armed with a knife, he wounded and killed one of Cao's brave and fierce generals, General Xia Houyuan. His victory decisively defeated the army of Cao and this made him very famous.

GAMES FOR FUN

Guess which weapon is used by Zhao Yun.

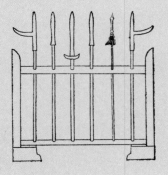

a spear

Answer:

Huā Mùlán
花木兰——
dài fù cóng jūn
代父从军

Hua Mulan – Serving the Army for her Father

Pre-reading Questions

1. Do you want to learn more about the first lady in ancient China to dress and disguise herself as a man?

2. Can you make a guess? Were there many heroines in ancient China?

3. In the eyes of the Chinese people, what had a lady in ancient China done in order for her to be looked upon as a heroine?

Hua Mulan

❶
     Huā Mùlán shì Zhōngguó zhùmíng de
     花 木 兰 是 中国 著名 的
nǚ yīngxióng
女 英雄。

❷
     Tā běnlái shì yī gè píngfán de
     她 本来 是 一 个 平凡 的
nǚháizi   Yǒu yī tiān wǎnshang tā zuò
女孩子。 有 一 天 晚上，她 坐
zài zhībùjī qiánmian   Fùqīn tīng dào
在 织布机 前面。 父亲 听 到

声音，以为她在织布，后来才发现那是她叹气的声音，父亲问她：“木兰，你在想什么呀？为什么

An ancient weaving machine

叹气呢？”木兰忧愁地说：“我没有在想什么，也不是在为自己发愁[1]。父亲呀，我昨天看到皇帝要大规模征兵的命令。命令已经发出很多道了，每一道命令上都有您的名字！父亲你年纪大了，又没有大儿子可以代你当兵，怎么办呢。我看只能由我去准备一切，让我代替您出征吧！”虽然父亲反对这样做，可是木兰坚持这样做，不断劝父亲，说自己应该为父亲分担[2]工作，父亲只好答应她。

GLOSSARY

1 发愁 worry
2 分担 share

Translation

❶　　　Hua Mulan was a famous heroine in China.

❷　　　Originally she was an ordinary girl. One evening she was sitting in front of the loom. Her father heard her and thought she was weaving cloth. Then he discovered that she was sighing. He asked, "Mulan! What were you thinking about? Why did you sigh?" Worriedly she replied, "I was not thinking of anything. I was not worried about myself either. Dad! Yesterday I saw a large-scale conscription order from the Emperor. Many orders have been issued and your name appeared on each of them. Dad! You are already quite old and you do not have an eldest son who is old enough to fulfill that conscription duty for you. How are we going to deal with this problem? I think I have to make all the preparations and perform that conscription duty for you." Although her father disagreed with her suggestion yet Mulan insisted on carrying out her plan. Incessantly she pleaded with her father saying that she should share the work with him. Finally he agreed to her suggestion.

❸
Dì　èr　tiān　Huā　Mùlán　dǎban　chéng　nánháizi　ránhòu
第 二 天 ，花 木 兰 打扮 成 男孩子 ，然后

tā　mǎshàng　jiù　qù　mǎi　mǎ　zhǔnbèi　wǔqì　hé　qítā
她 马上 就 去 买 马、 准备 武器 和 其他

zhuāngbèi　Tā　pǎo　biàn　le　zhěnggè　chéngshì　zhōngyú　mǎi　le
装备 。 她 跑 遍 了 整个 城市 ， 终于 买 了

yī　pǐ　hǎo　mǎ　hái　mǎi　qí　le　mǎbiān　mǎ'ān　děng
一 匹 好 马， 还 买 齐 了 马鞭、 马鞍 等

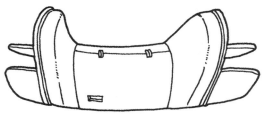

A saddle

装备，天亮了，木兰 依依 不 舍 地 与 父母
和 幼小 的 弟弟 妹妹 告别，跟随 军队 向
战场 出发。军队 日夜 赶路，经过 黄河，就
睡 在 黄河 边 上，木兰 再 不 能 听 到 父母
叫唤 她 的 声音，只 能 听 到 黄河 急促
的 流水 在 哗哗 地 流 的 声音，她 很 怀念
家人。第 二 天 还 得 离开 黄河，到 更
远 的 黑山 去，这 时 她 更 听 不 到 父母
的 声音 了，只 听 到 北方
敌人 的 战马 啾啾[3] 的
叫 声。军队 飞快
地 越 过 一 座
座 大 山，闯 过 一 道
道 关卡，经过 漫长 的
路途，打 过 一 次 又 一
次 的 仗。北方 的 夜晚

A warrior on horse

64

很 冷，木兰 和 伙伴 每 天 听 着 营地 里
报时 的 声音 入睡，冷冷 的 月光 照 在 他们
的 铁甲 战袍 上。为了 活 下来，为了 不 让
别人 发现 她 是 女孩，木兰 付 出 了 巨大 的
努力。十 多 年 里，军队 经过 了 无数 次
战斗，连 将军 都 死 在 战场 上。战争 终于
结束 了，木兰 和 活 下来 的 伙伴 成为 打 胜
仗 的 英雄，回 到 首都。

❹　皇帝 十分 高兴，要 赏赐⁴ 给 军队 的
英雄。花 木兰 有 很 大 的 功劳，皇帝 赏赐
了 很 多 财宝 给 她。皇帝 问 木兰 还 想 要
什么，木兰 说："我 不 想 做 大 官。我 希望
皇上 能 给 我 一 匹 千里马，让 我 早日 回
到 家乡，和 家人 在 一起。"

GLOSSARY

3 啾啾　a whiny voice

4 赏赐　reward

Translation

❸   The next day, Hua Mulan dressed herself as a man. Then she went immediately to buy a horse, and prepare her weapons and other equipment. She looked all over the city and finally she bought a really good horse and also all her other riding accessories like a horsewhip and a saddle. At dawn Mulan reluctantly said good-bye to her parents and her young brother and sister. She followed the army and headed towards the battlefield. They hurried all the way, all day and through the night. When they passed by the Yellow River (Huang He) they rested and slept by the river. Mulan could no longer hear the calling of her parents. She could only hear the sound of the rapid running water of the fast flowing Yellow River. She really missed her family, her parents and her siblings. The next day they had to leave the Yellow River and travel further to the Black Mountain (Hei Shan). By then it was even harder for her to hear the calling of her parents. She could only hear the whining of the battle horses of the northern enemy. With speed as fast as flying the army climbed over one large mountain after another. They rammed through one castle gate after another. They traveled a long way and fought one battle after another. The nights in the northern country were cold and Mulan and her comrades slept through those nights listening to the drumming sound that announced the time. The cold moonlight shone on their iron-armored battle robes. In order to stay alive and not to be discovered as a girl, Mulan made tremendous efforts. In those twelve long years the army went through a lot of fighting in numerous battles. Even the general died on the battlefield. At last the war ended. Mulan and her comrades who managed to survive became victorious war heroes. They returned to the capital.

❹   The Emperor was very happy with their victory and wanted to reward the war heroes. Because of her tremendous battle merits the Emperor rewarded Mulan with a lot of treasure. He asked Mulan what else did she want? Mulan said, "I do not want to serve as a high-ranking governing minister. I hope that your highness could give me a fast horse so that I could go home as quickly as possible to unite with my family."

❺

Dāng zhīdao nǚ'ér huílai de xiāoxi Mùlán de
当 知道 女儿 回来 的 消息，木兰 的

fùmǔ hùxiāng chānfú zhe dào chéng wài qù jiē tā Mùlán
父母 互相 搀扶[5] 着 到 城 外 去 接 她。 木兰

de jiějie tīng dào mèimei yào huílai mǎshàng dǎban
的 姐姐 听 到 妹妹 要 回来，马上 打扮

zìjǐ chuān de hěn piàoliang de qù yíngjiē tā Mùlán
自己，穿 得 很 漂亮 地 去 迎接 她。 木兰

de dìdi tīng dào jiějie yào huílai gāoxìng de bǎ dāo
的 弟弟 听 到 姐姐 要 回来，高兴 地 把 刀

mó de gèng fēnglì zhǔnbèi shā zhū shā yáng qìngzhù yī
磨 得 更 锋利，准备 杀 猪 杀 羊 庆祝 一

fān Mùlán huí dào zìjǐ de fángjiān tuō xia zhànpáo huàn
番。 木兰 回到 自己 的 房间，脱 下 战袍，换

shang nǚhái de yīshang Tā duì zhe chuānghu shū tóufa duì
上 女孩 的 衣裳。 她 对 着 窗户 梳 头发，对

zhe jìngzi zǐxì de huàzhuāng Dāng Mùlán zǒu chu fáng
着 镜子 仔细 地 化妆。 当 木兰 走 出 房

mén tā de nán zhànyǒu dōu shífēn jīngyà Wǒmen hé
门，她 的 男 战友 都 十分 惊讶：" 我们 和

nǐ yīqǐ shēnghuó yīqǐ zhàndòu le shí èr nián jìngrán
你 一起 生活，一起 战斗 了 十二 年，竟然

bù zhīdao nǐ shì yī gè nǚháizi Mùlán tiáopí de
不 知道 你 是 一个 女孩子！" 木兰 调皮 地

shuō Dāng xióng tù bèi zhuā zhu ěrduo tā de shuāng jiǎo huì
说：" 当 雄 兔 被 抓住 耳朵，它 的 双 脚 会

bù tíng bǎidòng cí tù jiù jīngcháng mī zhe yǎnjing Dànshì
不 停 摆动；雌 兔 就 经常 眯 着 眼睛。 但是

dāng xióngxìng tùzi hé cíxìng tùzi yīqǐ zài dì shang pǎo
当 雄性 兔子 和 雌性 兔子 一起 在 地上 跑

de shíhou nǐmen zěnnéng fēn chu nǎ zhī shì xióng tù nǎ
的 时候，你们 怎能 分 出 哪 只 是 雄 兔，哪

zhī shì cí tù ne
只 是 雌 兔 呢 ？"

❻ Mùlán wèile fùqīn ér bàn nánhái dǎzhàng de
木兰 为了 父亲 而 扮 男孩 打仗 的

shì lìng suǒyǒu zhīdao de rén dōu hěn pèifú yǒu gè
事，令 所有 知道 的 人 都 很 佩服，有 个

shīrén xiě le yī shǒu Mùlán shī jīhū suǒyǒu Zhōngguó
诗人 写 了 一 首 木兰 诗，几乎 所有 中国

xuésheng dōu dú guo zhè shǒu shī zhīdao zhège gùshi
学生 都 读 过 这 首 诗，知道 这个 故事。

GLOSSARY

5 搀扶 hold, support

Translation

❺ Hearing the news that their daughter was coming home, Mulan's aging parents held each other and made their way to outside the city to meet her. When Mulan's elder sister heard of Mulan's return she immediately dressed beautifully to go to welcome her home. When Mulan's younger brother heard that his sister was coming home he was so happy that he sharpened the knife, getting ready to slaughter some pigs and sheep to celebrate. Mulan went back to her room and took off her battle robe and put on a lady-like dress. Facing the window she combed her hair and she looked at herself in the mirror to carefully put on her makeup. When she walked out of her room her battle comrades were all very surprised and said, "How was it possible that we lived with you and fought battles with you for 12 years and we did not know that you are a girl?" Naughtily Mulan replied, "When a buck rabbit is lifted up into the air by the ears he struggles with the hind legs incessantly. When the same thing is done to a doe rabbit she usually only closes her eyes. But when they are allowed to run freely on the ground how can you distinguish which one is a buck rabbit and which one is a doe rabbit?"

❻   All the people who knew about Mulan disguising herself as a man to carry out the conscription duty of her father greatly respected her. A poet wrote a poem, called "Mulan Shi". Nearly all Chinese students have studied this poem and learned about this story.

Heroines in China

A lot of people may feel that the social status of women in ancient China was not very high. They had to obey men in everything and were restricted in their activities. But are you aware of the fact that there were many heroines in the history of China? They were highly skilled in martial arts, intelligent and brave. They fought side-by-side with men and won respect from everybody.

In the novel opera Mu Guiying was one of the famous generals in the Yang family. According to the legend, an immortal lady taught her the techniques of archery and knife throwing known only among the immortals. Once she annihilated the Tianmen battle formation of the State of Liao and defeated their army, earning a lot of military merits for herself.

As the chief general Fan Lihua led an army to defeat a rebellious gang to bring back social order. After her husband and his family were beheaded because of a wrongful conviction, she took her son and led the army to attack the capital, Chang'an. After getting in she killed the bad high-ranking minister who had framed her husband.

There were many similarly famous heroines in the history of China. One of them was known for her heroic act of riding a horse for several hundred miles in one night in order to inform her husband, who subsequently defeated a rebellious gang and restored the social order. There was another one who charged through the surrounding battle formation set up by the enemy in order to get help from a neighboring city, which sent an army to rescue her army. They have earned the respect of successive generations.

When you talk about heroines you cannot miss the one who performed the draft duty for her father, Hua Mulan. But while the other heroines fought their battles as women, Hua Mulan went to join the war disguised as a man. (In those days girls were not allowed in the army.).

GAMES FOR FUN

Please specify the sex of the following figures. Write M for male and F for female.

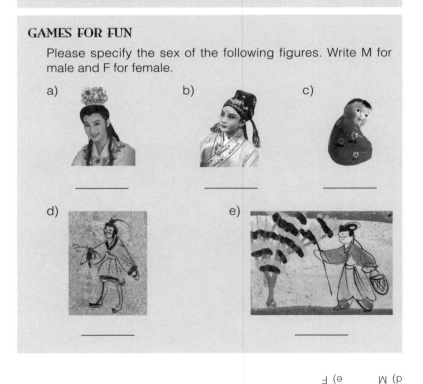

a)

b)

c)

d)

e)

Lǐ   Jìng   yǔ   Né   Zhā

李靖与哪吒

Li Jing and Ne Zha

Pre-reading Questions

1. How did a little immortal challenge the East Ocean Dragon King?
2. Do you think Ne Zha's teacher was mortal?

---

❶
Yībān rén dōu shì zài mǔqīn de dùzi li shí gè
一般 人 都 是 在 母亲 的 肚子 里 十 个

yuè jiù chūshēng kěshì Zhōngguó shénhuà li yǒu yī gè shàonián
月 就 出生，可是 中国 神话 里 有 一 个 少年

yīngxióng Né Zhā què zài mǔqīn de dùzi li dāi le sān
英雄 哪吒，却 在 母亲 的 肚子 里 待 了 三

nián liù gè yuè Né Zhā
年 六 个 月。 哪 吒

de fùqīn shì zhùmíng jiāngjūn
的 父亲 是 著名 将军

Lǐ Jìng Né Zhā bùdàn zài
李 靖。 哪 吒 不但 在

mǔqīn dùzi li de shíjiān
母亲 肚子 里 的 时间

cháng tā shēng xialai de
长， 他 生 下来 的

Ne Zha - the teenage hero

时候，是一个肉球，吓了大家一跳。正在大家手忙脚乱的时候，肉球突然发光，一个男孩从肉球里跳出来，他就是哪吒。李靖看着这个奇怪的儿子，闷闷不乐。他没有跟外面的人讲过哪吒出生的怪事。没想到有一个奇怪的人来祝贺，要求做哪吒的老师。他见孩子左手掌有个"哪"字，右手掌有个"吒"字，就为孩子起名哪吒，并且送他一件宝物：乾坤圈。哪吒跟两个哥哥比较起来，真是又聪明又顽皮，李靖对这个儿子是又爱又担心，怕他会闯祸。

Ne Zha's wheels of the wind and the fire.

Translation

❶   Most people are born after staying ten months inside their mother's womb. But in Chinese mythology there was a teenage hero, Ne Zha (as shown in the picture), who stayed three years and six months in his mother's womb before he was born. His father was a famous general, Li Jing. Not only was Ne Zha's prenatal period long but he was also born in the form of a meatball. Seeing this everyone was shocked and bustled around trying to deal with this unusual object. At that moment the meatball suddenly emitted light and a boy jumped out from the meatball. He was Ne Zha. Watching his strange son, Li Jing was depressed and not very happy. He had never told anyone the strange manner in which Ne Zha was born. Yet out of the blue a strange person came to congratulate him and he asked to be Ne Zha's teacher. He saw a Chinese character "Ne" in the boy's left palm and another Chinese character "Zha" on the right one. Then he gave the name "Ne Zha" to the boy. He also gave him a treasure called the Qiankunquan. Compared to his two elder brothers' behavior as children, Ne Zha was both very smart and very naughty. As much as Li Jing loved Ne Zha he was worried about him. He was afraid that Ne Zha would get into trouble.

❷

Hěn kuài Né Zhā zhǎng dào qī suì Bù zhīdao wèi shénme
很 快 哪 吒 长 到 七 岁。不 知 道 为 什 么,

zhè nián fùzé xiàyǔ de Dōnghǎi Lóngwáng yī dī yǔshuǐ yě
这 年 负 责 下 雨 的 东 海 龙 王 一 滴 雨 水 也

bù jiàng Yǒu yī tiān Né Zhā hé gēge qù Dōnghǎi wán Tā
不 降。有 一 天,哪 吒 和 哥 哥 去 东 海 玩。他

ná zhe Qiánkūn quān zài shuǐ li wán shí Dōnghǎi Lóngwáng
拿 着 乾 坤 圈 在 水 里 玩 时,东 海 龙 王

de wánggōng měngliè yáodòng Lóngwáng jímáng pài Yèchā qù
的 王 宫 猛 烈 摇 动。龙 王 急 忙 派 夜 叉 去

kàn Yèchā fāxiàn shì Né Zhā zài wán dà shēng zémà Nǐ
看,夜 叉 发 现 是 哪 吒 在 玩,大 声 责 骂:"你

shì nǎli lái de háizi gǎn dào
是 哪里 来 的 孩子，敢 到

Dōnghǎi dǎoluàn Né Zhā méiyǒu
东海 捣乱[1]！" 哪 吒 没有

shòu guo zhèyàng de zémà shēngqì
受 过 这样 的 责骂，生气

de shuō Dōnghǎi shì nǐ jiā de
地 说："东海 是 你 家 的

ma Jiù bùxǔ wǒmen lái wán
吗？就 不许 我们 来 玩

yīxià Yèchā shēnshǒu lái zhuā
一下？" 夜叉 伸手 来 抓

Ne Zha fought with his weapon, Qiankunquan

tā Né Zhā ná Qiánkūn quān jiù dǎ yīxiàzi jiù bǎ nàge
他，哪 吒 拿 乾坤 圈 就 打，一下子 就 把 那个

Yèchā dǎ sǐ le qítā Yèchā huāngmáng táozǒu bùliào
夜叉 打 死 了，其他 夜叉 慌忙 逃走，不料

cōngmáng zhōngzhuàng dǎo le Lóngwáng de sān tàizǐ Sān tàizǐ wèn
匆忙 中 撞 倒 了 龙王 的 三 太子。三 太子 问

míngbai qíngkuàng yào lìkè qù jiàoxùn Né Zhā jiéguǒ yě bèi
明白 情况，要 立刻 去 教训 哪 吒，结果 也 被

Né Zhā dǎ sǐ Lóngwáng hěn shāngxīn dǎsuan qù tiānshàng xiàng
哪 吒 打 死。龙王 很 伤心，打算 去 天上 向

Tiāndì gàozhuàng bù xiǎng bèi Né Zhā bàn lù lán zhu dǎ le
天帝 告状[2]，不 想 被 哪 吒 半 路 拦 住，打了

yī dùn Yúshì Dōnghǎi Lóngwáng qǐng lai xiōngdi Nánhǎi
一 顿。于是，东海 龙王 请 来 兄弟 —— 南海

Lóngwáng Xīhǎi Lóngwáng Běihǎi Lóngwáng shāngliang zěnyàng bàofù
龙王、西海 龙王、北海 龙王，商量 怎样 报复。

GLOSSARY

1 捣乱 make a lot of trouble
2 告状 complain against

Translation

❷   Very quickly Ne Zha grew up into a seven-year-old boy. For reasons unknown, the East Ocean Dragon King (as shown in the picture) who was responsible for creating rainfall would not make even one drop of rain. One day Ne Zha and his brothers went to play in the East Ocean. When he was holding his Qiankunquan to play in the water the palace of the East Ocean Dragon King rocked vigorously. The Dragon King quickly sent a Yecha (as shown in the picture; it is pronounced as Yaksha in the original Buddhist terminology and it is a malevolent spirit) to see what was happening. When that Yecha found out that Ne Zha and his brothers were playing there he loudly scolded them, "Where do you boys come from? You dare to come to the East Ocean to make trouble!" Ne Zha had never been scolded like that before and angrily replied, "Is the East Ocean your home? Why are we not allowed to play here for a while?" The Yecha wanted to grab him with his hands. Ne Zha took up his Qiankunquan and struck him, killing the Yecha instantly with only one strike. The other Yechas were scared and ran off in such a hurry that they knocked over the third prince of the Dragon King. After learning what had happened the third prince immediately went to teach Ne Zha a lesson. Consequently he was also killed. The East Ocean Dragon King was greatly saddened by this and he planned to file a complaint to the Heavenly Emperor. Unexpectedly, halfway there he was blocked and beaten up by Ne Zha. Then the East Ocean Dragon King invited his brothers, the South Ocean Dragon King, the West Ocean Dragon King, and the North Ocean Dragon King, to plan a strategy for revenge.

❸ 第二天，四个龙王
发大水淹了李靖住的
地方，要李靖交出哪
吒。哪吒想反击，却被
父亲拦住，乾坤圈也被
父亲收去。眼看水越来
越高，全城的人快要淹

"The Pagoda Holding Heavenly King Li" cupped Ne Zha under a pagoda. This is what an ancient pagoda looks like

死了。哪吒于是对龙王和李靖说："我
的命是父母给的，要我死，我的命
也只能还给父母，不能给龙王！"说
完，他拔刀自杀，把肉割下还给
母亲，把骨还给父亲。哪吒死后，他的
老师拿莲藕做骨，拿莲叶做肉，使哪吒
复活³，又送给他更多宝物。

❹ 虽然复活了，哪吒还是恨父亲，要
杀父亲报仇。李靖打不过儿子，幸好佛

<table>
<tr><td>lái</td><td>bāngmáng</td><td>Fó</td><td>sòng</td><td>yī</td><td>zuò</td><td>bǎotǎ</td><td>gěi</td><td>Lǐ</td><td>Jìng</td><td>jiāng</td><td>Né</td></tr>
<tr><td>来</td><td>帮忙。</td><td>佛</td><td>送</td><td>一</td><td>座</td><td>宝塔</td><td>给</td><td>李</td><td>靖，</td><td>将</td><td>哪</td></tr>
</table>

来帮忙。佛送一座宝塔给李靖，将哪

吒罩在塔里，李靖从此叫做"托塔李

天王"。后来，佛劝李靖放了哪吒，父子

两人才和解⁴。哪吒可以变成有三个

头，六只手，又有老师送的宝物，能力

很大。每一次李靖打仗，哪吒都会去

帮父亲的忙。

GLOSSARY

3 复活 regain one's life; be reborn   4 和解 reconcile

Translation

❸　　The next day the four Dragon Kings sent a lot of water to flood the place where Li Jing lived. Ne Zha wanted to strike back but his action was blocked by his father, who even took away his Qiankunquan. Seeing that the water level was rising higher and higher and the people of the whole town would soon be drowned, Ne Zha said to the Dragon Kings and Li Jing, "My life was given to me by my parents. If you want me to die my life can only be returned to them not to you and your dragon brothers." After saying this he took out his knife and killed himself. Then he cut up his muscles and returned them to his mother and returned the bones to his father. After his death Ne Zha's teacher revived him by using lotus roots to create bones and lotus leaves to create muscles.

❹　　Although Ne Zha regained his life he still hated his father and wanted to kill him for revenge. In the fight Li Jing was losing to his son. Luckily for him Buddha came to the rescue. He gave Li Jing a treasure pagoda as a gift, which was used by Li Jing to cover Ne Zha. From then on Li Jing has been called "The Pagoda Holding Heavenly King Li"(as shown in the picture). Later on Buddha advised Li Jing to release Ne Zha and both father and son then reconciled. Ne Zha had great power. Besides being armed with the treasure from his teacher he could turn himself into a being with three heads and six arms. Every time Li Jing went to fight a battle Ne Zha would go to help him.

Expansion Reading

The Four Ocean Dragon Kings

According to Chinese mythology, the four Ocean Dragon Kings are the governors of the oceans, responsible for the management and welfare of all undersea creatures. The four Ocean Dragon Kings govern the four parts of the undersea world, the northern, southern, eastern and western parts. (In Chinese 四方 can mean the four cardinal points on a compass, north, south, east and west, or it can mean a square. Here it literally means the four directions.). The four Ocean Dragon Kings appear in both *Journey to the West* and *Feng Shen Yan Yi, Epic Stories of Chinese Mythology*. According to mythology, young Ocean Dragon Kings can be present in all regions of the Oceans. They all have the appearance of a dragon head and a human body.

The Ocean Dragon Kings live in Dragon Palaces at the bottom of their respective Oceans, and their undersea territories are under their complete command. The bottom of the ocean is a mysterious place for the immortals, beautiful and rich with uncountable treasures. The Dragon Palaces were built with completely transparent blocks of crystal. They are extremely beautiful. The fish, prawns, crabs, turtles and other creatures have supernatural abilities. They are the generals and soldiers serving under the

The East Ocean Dragon King and his brothers

Ocean Dragon Kings. When Ne Zha was making trouble in the East Ocean they came out to fight and defend the Dragon Palace.

Some people believed that the Ocean Dragon Kings were related to the amount of rainfall. They could also summon the lighting god, the thunder god, the wind god and the rain god to act according to their commands. Droughts and periods of heavy rainfall are some of the manifestations of their wrath to punish ordinary people. To pray for normal weather with regular wind and rain patterns, Ocean Dragon King Temples have been built to worship them, begging them to govern the water element properly and give people normal weather with rainfall and wind patterns that are conducive to agricultural abundance.

GAMES FOR FUN

Please match Ne Zha's treasure and its function(s).

Treasure	Function
a) Qiankunquan	1) tie up his enemy
b) rope	2) change its size and throw it at his enemy
c) spear	3) attack his enemy

Answers:
a) —— 1)
b) —— 2)
c) —— 3)

Yuè   Fēi
岳飞 ——

dà   pò   Jīn   bīng
大破金兵

**Yue Fei – the Hero Who
Decisively Defeated the
Army of the State of Jing**

Yue Fei – the hero who
defended the country and
protected the people of the
State of Song against the
State of Jing

Pre-reading Questions

1. Can you make a guess as to the kind of accessories used to equip horses to fight battles in ancient China?

2. What is a cattle and sheep-raising nomadic tribe good at?

---

❶
Yuè   Fēi   gōngyuán   nián   shì Zhōngguó
岳 飞 （公元 1103 — 1142 年）是 中 国

zuìjìn   yī qiān nián zuì yǒumíng de wèi guó yīngxióng   Tā
最 近 一 千 年 最 有 名 的 卫 国 英 雄。 他

bǎowèi guójiā rénmín jiéguǒ bèi huángdì hé huàirén shāhài
保卫 国家 人民，结果 被 皇帝 和 坏人 杀害

de   bēijù[1]   bèi rén xiě chéng chàngxiāo gùshi shū suǒyǐ
的 悲剧[1]，被 人 写 成 畅销 故事 书，所以

lián xiǎoháizi dōu zhīdao tā   Yuè Fēi xiǎo shíhou xuéxí
连 小孩子 都 知道 他。 岳 飞 小 时候 学习

wǔshù   shì yǒumíng de wǔshù gāoshǒu   Tā hái xǐhuan dú
武术，是 有名 的 武术 高手。 他 还 喜欢 读

lìshǐ   dǒngde xǔduō dài bīng dǎzhàng de fāngfǎ
历史，懂得 许多 带 兵 打仗 的 方法。

❷ 当时 中国 的 北方 已经 被 金国
占领，宋 朝 把 首都 搬 到 长江 南面。金
是 游牧 人 建立 的，擅长² 骑马 和 射箭。金
想 把 宋 朝 消灭 掉。宋 朝 也 想 把 北方 的
土地 拿 回来，宋 和 金 常常 打仗。

❸ 岳 飞 参加 军队，对抗 金国。他 作战
非常 勇敢，很 快 便 升 为 将军。岳 飞 的
军队 纪律 很 严，称 为 "岳 家 军"。"岳 家
军" 从来 都 不 影响 老百姓 的 生活，士兵
晚上 也 只是 睡 在 老百姓 的 屋 外，请 他们
进 屋 休息，他们 也 不 进去。岳 家 军
训练 严格，作战 很 勇敢，金国 的 士兵 常常
说："要 推 倒 一 座 山 很 容易，但 想 推 倒
岳 家 军 就 很 困难 啊！"

GLOSSARY

1 悲剧   tragedy
2 擅长   be good at

Translation

❶   Yue Fei (1103 – 1142 A.D.) was the most famous national hero in the last one thousand years of Chinese history. He defended the country and protected the people. Unfortunately, his heroic deeds ended tragically with him being killed by the Emperor and other bad people. Based on this tragedy popular storybooks have been written and as a result even small children know about him. When he was young, Yue Fei studied martial arts and was a famous and very skillful martial artist. He also liked to study history and knew a lot of methods of how to lead an army in fighting different kinds of battles.

❷   At that time northern China had already been occupied by the State of Jing. The Song Government moved its capital to the south side of the Yangtze River (the area called Chang Jiang in Chinese). The State of Jing had been established by a nomadic tribe whose members were very good at horseback riding and archery. The State of Jing wanted to annihilate the State of Song, which wanted to recover the northern territories taken away by the State of Jing. Wars frequently broke out between the two states.

❸   Yue Fei joined the army to defend the country against the State of the Jing. In battles he was very brave and he was quickly promoted to be a general. Yue Fei's army was under strict discipline and was called the "Army of the Yue Family", it was to never infringe on the lives of ordinary people. At night the soldiers only slept outside the houses of the ordinary people, who sometimes invited the soldiers to rest inside the house. They would decline the offer. The "Army of the Yue Family" had undergone very strict training and it fought bravely in battles. The soldiers of the State of Jing frequently said, "It is easy to topple a mountain. It is very difficult to topple the Army of the Yue Family."

❹
Gōngyuán 公元 1140 nián 年，
Jīnguó yòu yī cì chūbīng
金国 又 一 次 出兵
dǎ Sòngguó dài bīng de
打 宋国，带 兵 的
rén shì Jīnguó wángzǐ
人 是 金国 王子。
Tā xùnliàn le yī zhī hěn
他 训练 了 一 支 很
tèbié de qíbīng shìbīng
特别 的 骑兵，士兵

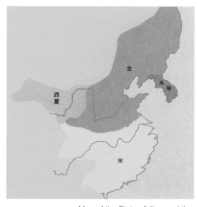

Map of the State of Jing and the State of Song

ná chángqiāng zhànmǎ dōu pī shang hòuhòu de tiějiǎ mìnglìng
拿 长枪，战马 都 披 上 厚厚 的 铁甲，命令
yīxià jiù chōng xiàng dírén Yóuyú qíbīng de sùdù hěn
一下 就 冲 向 敌人。由于 骑兵 的 速度 很
kuài shā shāng lì yòu dà érqiě suǒyǒu mǎ dōu pī shang
快，杀 伤 力 又 大，而且 所有 马 都 披 上
le tiějiǎ yīncǐ hěn nán shānghài dào tāmen Sòngguó de
了 铁甲，因此 很 难 伤害 到 它们。宋国 的
jūnduì dōu bèi Jīnguó dǎbài le shīqù hěn duō chéngshì hé
军队 都 被 金国 打败 了，失去 很 多 城市 和
tǔdì
土地。

❺
Sòngguó de huángdì jímáng pài Yuè Fēi dài jūn dǐdǎng
宋国 的 皇帝 急忙 派 岳 飞 带 军 抵挡。
Yuè Fēi jiē dào mìnglìng hòu mǎshàng chūfā Tā zhīdao
岳 飞 接 到 命令 后 马上 出发。他 知道
Jīnguó yǒu yī duì hěn lìhai de tiějiǎ qíbīng bīngqì kǎn
金国 有 一 队 很 厉害 的 铁甲 骑兵，兵器 砍
zài mǎ shēn shang dōu shāng bù liǎo mǎ yúshì biàn kǔkǔ xiǎng
在 马 身 上 都 伤 不 了 马，于是 便 苦苦 想

bànfǎ   xiāomiè   zhè   zhī   jūnduì
办法 消灭 这 支 军队。

❻ Dì   èr   tiān   dǎzhàng   de   shíhou   Jīnguó   wángzǐ   qīnzì
第 二 天 打仗 的 时候，金国 王子 亲自

dàilǐng   tiějiǎ   qíbīng   chōngfēng   tā   rènwéi   xiàng   yǐqián   yīyàng
带领 铁甲 骑兵 冲锋，他 认为 像 以前 一样，

hěn   kuài   jiù   néng   qǔshèng   zěn   zhīdao   kuài   chōng   dào   Yuè   jiā   jūn
很 快 就 能 取胜，怎 知道 快 冲 到 岳家军

shí   Yuè   jiā   jūn   zhōng   yīzhèn   gǔ   shēng   yī   pái   shìbīng   ná   dài
时，岳家军 中 一阵 鼓声，一 排 士兵 拿 带

gōu   de   chángqiāng   yīqí   gōu   xiàng   tiějiǎ   qíbīng   de   mǎjiǎo
钩 的 长枪，一齐 钩 向 铁甲 骑兵 的 马脚。

❼ Yuánlái   qíbīng   suīrán   shēn   pī   tiějiǎ   dàn   mǎjiǎo
原来 骑兵 虽然 身 披 铁甲，但 马脚

méiyǒu   rènhé   bǎohù   yuè   fēi   jiù   shì   kàn   dào   dírén
没有 任何 保护，岳 飞 就 是 看 到 敌人

zhège   ruòdiǎn[3]   mìnglìng   shìbīng   zhìzào   le   yī   pī   dài   gōu
这个 弱点[3]，命令 士兵 制造 了 一 批 带 钩

de   chángqiāng   zài   zhànchǎng   shang   zhuānmén   duìfu   mǎjiǎo   Shāng
的 长枪，在 战场 上 专门 对付 马脚。 伤

le   jiǎo   de   mǎ   hé   mǎ   shang   de   qíbīng   biàn   yīqǐ   dǎo   zài
了 脚 的 马 和 马 上 的 骑兵 便 一起 倒 在

dì   shang   Yuè   jiā   jūn   chéng   shèng   gōngjī   zhè   zhī   céng   shì
地 上，岳 家 军 乘 胜 攻击，这 支 曾 是

tiānxià   wúdí[4]   de   tiějiǎ   qíbīng   hěn   kuài   jiù   bài   xialai
天下 无敌[4] 的 铁甲 骑兵 很 快 就 败 下来

le   Jīnguó   de   wángzǐ   dài   zhe   jūnduì   táozǒu   le
了。金国 的 王子 带 着 军队 逃走 了。

Glossary

3 弱点 weakness
4 无敌 invincible

Translation

❹   In 1140 A.D. the State of Jing again sent an army, led by her prince, to attack the State of Song. He had trained a very special cavalry. All the cavaliers carried long spears. Their battle horses were all draped with thick iron armor. Whenever they were ordered to they would charge at the enemy. Because of the fast speed of the cavalry, the great ability of the soldiers to inflict casualties, and the iron armored horses, it was very hard to hurt them. Nearly all the armies of the State of Song were defeated by the State of Jing, and they lost a lot of cities and land to the enemy. The Song Emperor quickly sent Yue Fei to lead an army to defend against them.

❺   Receiving the order Yue Fei went immediately. He knew the State of Jing had a formidable iron-armored cavalry. The bodies of the horse were immune to any injuries inflicted by weapons. Then he thought very hard in his mind looking for a way to destroy this cavalry.

❻   The next day in a battle the prince of the State of Jing personally led the ironclad cavalry to charge at his enemy. He thought his victory would come quickly as usual. He could never have imagined what happened just when they were about to reach the "Army of the Yue Family", some members of which had started beating the drums. A line of soldiers, each carrying a long spear with a hook, appeared and in unison they used the hooks to trip the legs of the iron-armored cavalry.

❼   This was the weakness, observed by Yue Fei, of his enemy. Although members of the cavalry were draped with iron armor, the legs of the horses were unprotected. He ordered the soldiers to make a number of long spears with hooks, these were special to be used to deal with the legs of the horses in battle. After the leg injuries, the horses and the cavaliers on the horses fell to the ground. The "Army of the Yue Family" used this as an advantage in the attack for a great victory. The once invincible ironclad cavalry was quickly defeated and the prince of the State of Jing led his army to run away.

❽

Yuè jiā jūn yīzhí qiánjìn, dírén zhǐyào tīng dào
岳　家　军　一直　前进，敌人　只要　听　到

Yuè Fēi de míngzi biàn huì táozǒu Sòngguó jiēlián shōuhuí
岳　飞　的　名字　便　会　逃走，宋国　接连　收回

xǔduō chéngshì hé tǔdì Yuè Fēi yě yīncǐ chéngwéi zhùmíng
许多　城市　和　土地。岳　飞　也　因此　成为　著名

de kàng Jīn yīngxióng Kěshì Sòng de huángdì hé huài de
的　抗　金　英雄。可是，宋　的　皇帝　和　坏　的

dàchén bù xiǎng dǎzhàng yào hé Jīn hétán Jīnguó wángzǐ
大臣　不　想　打仗，要　和　金　和谈。金国　王子

yào xiān shā Yuè Fēi cái dāyìng hétán Yúshì huángdì
要　先　杀　岳　飞，才　答应　和谈。于是　皇帝

mìnglìng Yuè Fēi lìjí shōubīng děng Yuè Fēi huílai hòu biàn
命令　岳　飞　立即　收兵，等　岳　飞　回来　后，便

yòng Mòxūyǒu de zuìmíng shā le tā
用"莫须有"的　罪名　杀　了　他。

Translation

❽　　The "Army of the Yue Family" kept on advancing. Whenever the enemy heard the name of Yue Fei they would run away. One after another the State of Song regained many cities and pieces of land. As a result Yue Fei became the famous hero who defended the Song against the State of Jing. But the Song Emperor and some bad high-ranking ministers did not want to continue the war. They wanted to make peace with the State of Jing, the prince of which demanded that Yue Fei be killed first before he would promise to start peace negotiations. Then the Emperor ordered Yue Fei to retreat immediately. After his return he was executed with the charge of "No specific charge is necessary".

The State Of Jing

Why was Yue Fei the only person who could and did defeat the strong ironclad cavalry trained in the State of Jing? The State of Jing as a nation (1115 to 1234 A.D.) was established by a tribe called the Nu Zhen. The Nu Zhen tribe lived in the north and because of the cold weather they wore animal furs as their clothes. The region they lived in was rich in natural resources. Besides northern pearl, ginseng herbs, and pine nuts there were a lot of horses. Therefore they were all highly skilled in horsemanship.

After the leader of the Nu Zhen tribe had united all the smaller tribes he established the State of Jing, which mainly used the cavalry in fighting battles. The mounted soldiers of the cavalry were equipped with bows and arrows, long-handled horse knives and even sticks that were armor-clad and had the teeth of wolves. Their usual tactic was to use a bilateral wing-like battle formation. This was formed by the specialized cavalry of iron-clad horses. They were strong and mobile due to their use of horse power, and could stage sudden attacks. They were best at carrying out strategic plans which included unexpected attacks from a long distance and outflanking their enemy.

Later on the State of Jing defeated the State of Song, which has been called Bei (meaning north in Chinese) Song by Chinese historians. The royal family of Bei Song was forced to retreat to the region south of the Yangtze River, which was called Chang Jiang, after the name of the river. They established the State of Nan (meaning south in Chinese) Song and continued their defense against attacks from the State of Jing. There were many battles fought between the State of Jing and the State of Nan Song but because of the approximate equality in military power and strategic factors, neither one could decisively defeat the other, forming a stalemate which lasted for a long period of time. The State of Jing lasted over 120 years, ruling a vast region of the northern territories of China. Later on her strength as a nation weakened and the State of Jing was annihilated by the united army of the Mongols and the State of Nan Song in 1234 A.D.

Sūn　Wùkōng

孙悟空——

dà　nào　tiāngōng

大闹天宫

Sun Wukong – Creates Havoc at the Heavenly Palace

Sun Wukong wearing his tiger fur coat

Pre-reading Questions

1. Can you imagine what would happen if a monkey, which loves to eat and to play, barges into a banquet with a lot of food?

2. What kind of animal would you like to represent yourself with? The Chinese zodiac has twelve animals, including the monkey. Would you choose a monkey?

---

❶

Sūn Wùkōng shì yī zhī cóng shítou li shēng chulai
孙 悟空 是 一 只 从 石头 里 生 出来

de hóuzi Tā xuéxí le yī shēn běnlǐng dǒngde
的 猴子。 他 学习 了 一 身 本领, 懂得

xǔduō fǎshù[1] Tā dào hǎi li ná le Lóngwáng
许多 法术[1]。 他 到 海 里, 拿 了 龙王

yī jiàn bǎowù Jīngāngbàng huí dào tā zhù de
一 件 宝物 —— 金刚棒, 回 到 他 住 的

Huāguǒshān Lóngwáng yīnwèi shīqù le bǎowù fēicháng
花果山。 龙王 因为 失去 了 宝物, 非常

fènnù biàn xiàng Tiāndì gàozhuàng Tiāndì xiǎng chu yī
愤怒, 便 向 天帝 告状。 天帝 想 出 一

gè bànfǎ tā bǎ Sūn Wùkōng jiào dào tiānshàng ràng tā
个 办法, 他 把 孙 悟空 叫 到 天上, 让 他

zuò　yī　gè　guǎnlǐ　mǎ　de　guān　hǎo　ràng　Sūn　Wùkōng　bù
做 一 个 管 理 马 的 官 ，好 让 孙 悟 空 不

yào　zài　dǎoluàn　Sūn　Wùkōng　hěn　gāoxìng　měi　tiān　hǎohǎo
要 再 捣 乱 。 孙 悟 空 很 高 兴 ，每 天 好 好

guǎnlǐ　tā　de　mǎ　Kěshì　yǒu　yī　tiān　tā　wúyì² zhōng
管 理 他 的 马 。 可 是 有 一 天 ，他 无 意² 中

zhīdao　zìjǐ　zuò　de　shì　gè　xiǎo　guān　yī　nù　zhī
知 道 自 己 做 的 是 个 小 官 ，一 怒 之

xià　huí　dào　Huāguǒshān　shuō　zìjǐ　shì　Tiāndì　yīyàng　de
下 ，回 到 花 果 山 ，说 自 己 是 天 帝 一 样 的

dàiwáng　jiàozuò　Qítiāndàshèng
大 王 ，叫 做 ："齐 天 大 圣 "。

Glossary

1 法术　magical tricks
2 无意　by chance

Translation

❶　　Sun Wukong was a monkey born from a stone. He learned to command many supernatural powers with his body and knew many magical tricks. He went into the ocean and took away one of the Dragon King's treasures, the Jinggangbang (stick), and returned to his residence, Huaguoshan (a mountain). Because of the loss of the treasure the Dragon King became very angry. He filed a complaint to the Heavenly Emperor, who thought out a solution. He summoned Sun Wukong to Heaven and appointed him to be the officer for managing the horses so that he would be kept from making more trouble. Sun Wukong was very happy with the job and everyday he would take very good care of his horses. But one day he accidentally learned that the position given to him was ranked as a minor officer. Immediately he became very angry and returned to Huaguoshan. He said that he was a Great King, as equal in status as the Heavenly Emperor. He called himself, "The Heavenly High Great Holiness, Qitiandasheng".

❷ 天帝 很 生气，派
兵 去 捉 孙 悟空。但
孙 悟空 非常 有 本领，
他 打败 了 所有 来 捉
他 的 天神。天神 只好
逃 回 天上。天帝 没有
办法，承认 孙 悟空 可以
叫做 " 齐天大圣 "。天帝
又 怕 孙 悟空 整天³

Sun Wukong, the "Qitiandasheng,
the Heavenly High Great Holiness"

没 事 做，会 出 问题，于是 便 叫 他 管理
桃 园。

❸ 孙 悟空 是 一 只 猴子，喜欢 吃 桃，
而且 他 听说，吃 了 天上 桃 园 里 的 桃 能
长生 不 老，于是 便 偷偷 挑 了 又 大 又 熟
的 桃 来 吃。不 知 不 觉，桃 园 里 的 桃
几乎 都 被 孙 悟空 吃 光 了。有 一 天，天上

要 举行 宴会，派 人 到 桃 园 摘 桃。 孙
悟空 那 时 刚 吃 饱，变 得 小小 的，睡 在
桃 上。 摘 桃 的 人 正好 选 中 了 孙 悟空 睡
的 那个 桃，惊醒 了 孙 悟空。 他 立刻 变 回
原来 的 样子，手 里 还 拿 着 棒，吓 得 摘
桃 的 人 大 叫 起来。 孙 悟空 听 摘 桃 的 人
说 要 举行 宴会，请 了 许多 神仙，就是 没有
请 他，生气 得 不 得了。 他 决定 在 宴会
之 前 去 吃 掉 食物，还 把 剩 下 的 食物 都
装 进 袋 里 带 走。 但 因为 他 喝 了 很 多
酒，认 错 了 路，竟然 闯 进 天帝 放 仙 药 的
地方，把 专 给 天帝 吃 的 仙 药 当 炒 豆子
一样 都 吃 光 了，然后 才 回去 花果山。

Glossary

3 整天 for a whole day

Translation

❷   The Heavenly Emperor was greatly angered and sent his heavenly soldiers to go to arrest Sun Wukong. But Sun Wukong was extraordinarily armed with supernatural abilities. He defeated all the heavenly gods who were sent to capture him. Without any alternative the heavenly gods could only run back to Heaven. Without any other solution the Heavenly Emperor conceded to Sun Wukong's proclamation to call himself, "The Heavenly High Great Holiness, Qitiandasheng". Then the Heavenly Emperor asked Sun Wukong to manage the peach garden to keep him occupied so that he would not cause problems out of boredom from the idleness of doing nothing everyday.

❸   Sun Wukong was a monkey and like any monkey he liked to eat peaches. Moreover, he had heard that one could live forever after eating the peaches from the peach garden in Heaven. Secretly he picked the big and ripe peaches to eat. Gradually and unnoticeably nearly all the peaches in the peach garden in Heaven were eaten up by Sun Wukong. One day a banquet was going to be held in Heaven. People were sent to pick peaches in the peach garden. Sun Wukong had just eaten and, after shrinking himself into a very small Sun Wukong, he slept on a peach. The peach picker picked the very one on which Sun Wukong was sleeping. He was awakened and immediately turned himself back to his original appearance, carrying a stick in his hands. The peach picker was greatly frightened and screamed out loudly. When Sun Wukong heard that a banquet was going to be held and many immortals, except him, had been invited he became very very angry and decided to go and eat up all the food before the banquet would be held. After doing so he put all the leftover food into a bag to be taken away. But because he had drunk a lot of wine, he could not recognize the way back. He took the wrong path and subsequently barged into the place where the immortal medicine for the Heavenly Emperor was stored. As if eating fried beans, he ate up all the immortal medicine made especially for the Heavenly Emperor and then he returned to Huaguoshan.

④

Tiāndì zhīdao hòu fēicháng shēngqì, mìnglìng tiānjiàng
天帝 知道 后 非常 生气，命令 天将

dàilǐng shí wàn tiānbīng zài qù zhuō Sūn Wùkōng。 Tiānbīng
带领 十 万 天兵 再 去 捉 孙 悟空。 天兵

tiānjiàng lái dào Huāguǒshān wéigōng⁴ Sūn Wùkōng, cóng zǎoshang
天将 来 到 花果山 围攻⁴ 孙 悟空，从 早上

yīzhí dǎ dào wǎnshang。 Zuìhòu, Sūn Wùkōng cóng shēn shang
一直 打 到 晚上。 最后，孙 悟空 从 身 上

zhuā le yī dà bǎ máo, yòng kǒu yī chuī, měi tiáo máo biàn
抓 了 一 大 把 毛，用 口 一 吹，每 条 毛 变

chéng yī gè Sūn Wùkōng, dǎ de suǒyǒu tiānbīng tiānjiàng dōu
成 一 个 孙 悟空，打 得 所有 天兵 天将 都

táopǎo le。 Yúshì Sūn Wùkōng jìxù zài Huāguǒshān zuò tā
逃跑 了。 于是 孙 悟空 继续 在 花果山 做 他

de "Qítiāndàshèng"。
的 "齐天大圣"。

GLOSSARY

4 围攻 besiege

Stealing peaches from the Garden of Heaven

Translation

④   Knowing this, the Heavenly Emperor became very angry and ordered 100,000 heavenly soldiers led by heavenly generals to go to arrest Sun Wukong again. The heavenly soldiers and their generals came to Huaguoshan. They surrounded Sun Wukong and attacked him. They fought from dawn to dusk. At last Sun Wukong pulled out a bunch of hair from his body and blewon it with his mouth. Each piece of his hair was turned into another Sun Wukong. All the heavenly soldiers and heavenly generals were defeated and they ran away. Then Sun Wukong continued to stay on Huaguoshan as "The Heavenly High Great Holiness, Qitiandasheng", the title which he proclaimed himself.

The Supernatural Abilities of Sun Wukong

Journey to the West is one of the four famous classic novels in China. It was edited into a novel in the Ming Dynasty (1368 to 1644 A.D.) The story of *Journey to the West* was based on the actual long journey made by the eminent monk Xuan Zang in the Tang Dynasty. He made that journey to India to learn Buddhism and to bring home to China the Scriptures of Buddhism (sutras). The novel tells the story of how Sun Wukong protects the eminent monk Xuan Zang all the way to the Western Heaven to get the Scriptures and how he experienced 81 episodes of destined calamities.

Sun Wukong is the major character in *Journey to the West*. He is also called the Beautiful Monkey King and "Qitiandasheng, the Heavenly High Great Holiness". He is a spiritual monkey born out of a spiritual stone in the Huaguoshan. He has a pair of fiery red eyes with gold colored pupils, which can identify evil monsters in one look. He has 72 alternatives in mutation. He frequently changes himself into different things in order to scout for the enemy and to attack and destroy

Sun Wukong with a
gourd-shaped bottle

their dens. With one somersault he can travel eighteen thousand miles. He can also go up to heaven and travel underground. He can make dragons and tigers surrender to him. He is not afraid of Heaven and not afraid of Earth. He dares to declare war against the Heavenly Emperor and creates havoc at the Heavenly Palace. He also dares to compete with many evil spirits, ghosts and monsters. Sun Wukong is naughty but kindhearted. No matter how many times Xuan Zang misunderstands him, he does not give up his job of protecting him all the way on his journey to the Western Heaven.

The background of *Journey to the West* is very heavy in Buddhism. Some people thought that the model of Sun Wukong originated in the Holy Monkey of India. In the Indian epic poem "Luo Mo Yan Na", written in the fifth century B.C., there was a Holy Monkey, called Ha Nu Man.

GAMES FOR FUN

1. On the following picture, please label the special feature(s) of the model of Sun Wukong: a monkey face, the Jinggangquan(metal headband), the Jinggangbang (stick).

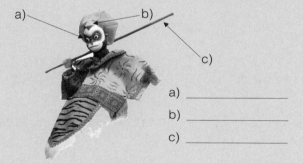

a) _____

b) _____

c) _____

2. Please draw a somersault cloud.

Wǔ Sōng dǎ hǔ

武松打虎

Wu Song – the Bare-handed Tiger Killer

Pre-reading Questions

1. It is common for people to die when they are attacked by a tiger. But it is very rare for anyone to kill a tiger with their bare hands. Do you want to learn more about this person?

2. What do the tigers of China look like?

❶ Wǔ Sōng yào gǎnlù huí gùxiāng Yī tiān zhōngwǔ tā
武 松 要 赶 路 回 故 乡。 一 天 中 午，他
zǒu de dùzi è le jiàn dào shāngǎng qián yǒu yī jiā
走 得 肚 子 饿 了，见 到 山 岗 前 有 一 家
jiǔjiā ménkǒu yǒu yī miàn qí xiě zhe Sān wǎn bù guò
酒 家，门 口 有 一 面 旗，写 着 "三 碗 不 过
gǎng
岗"。

❷ Wǔ Sōng jìnqu hē le yī wǎn jiǔ jué de jiǔ
武 松 进 去，喝 了 一 碗 酒，觉 得 酒
hěn hǎo yòu jiào le liǎng jīn niúròu lái xiàjiǔ Kěshì
很 好，又 叫 了 两 斤 牛 肉 来 下 酒。 可 是
Wǔ Sōng hē le sān wǎn jiǔ zhī hòu diàn zhǔrén jiù bù kěn
武 松 喝 了 三 碗 酒 之 后，店 主 人 就 不 肯

tiān jiǔ le   tā shuō yībān rén hē zhè zhǒng jiǔ sān wǎn
添 酒 了，他 说 一 般 人 喝 这 种 酒 三 碗

biàn zuì guò bù liǎo qiánmian de shāngǎng Kěshì Wǔ Sōng
便 醉，过 不 了 前 面 的 山 岗。可 是 武 松

zìshì jiǔliàng dà jiéguǒ qiánhòu hē le shí bā wǎn Dāng
自恃¹ 酒 量 大，结 果 前 后 喝 了 十 八 碗。当

tā fù le qián ná le suíshēn de bàng zhèngyào chūmén
他 付 了 钱，拿 了 随 身 的 棒，正 要 出 门

de shíhou diàn zhǔrén jímáng gàosu tā shān shang yǒu
的 时 候，店 主 人 急 忙 告 诉 他，山 上 有

lǎohǔ shānghài le èr sān shí rén zhèngfǔ yǐjing chū le
老 虎，伤 害 了 二 三 十 人，政 府 已 经 出 了

gàoshì yīncǐ guò shāngǎng yīdìng yào jiébàn tóngxíng Wǔ
告 示，因 此 过 山 岗 一 定 要 结 伴 同 行。武

Sōng zài fùjìn zhǎngdà xiǎo shíhou zhè shān zǒu guo hěn duō
松 在 附 近 长 大，小 时 候 这 山 走 过 很 多

cì méi tīng guo yǒu lǎohǔ bù kěn tīng diàn zhǔrén de
次，没 听 过 有 老 虎，不 肯 听 店 主 人 的

huà xiàng shāngǎng dàbù zǒu qu
话，向 山 岗 大 步² 走 去。

GLOSSARY

1 自恃 self-confident
2 大步 in great strides

Translation

❶   Wu Song had to hurry back to his old hometown village. One day at noon he had walked so much that he felt hungry. He saw a restaurant that served wine in front of a hill, at the gate of which there was a flag with a slogan written on it, saying, "No one should cross over the hill after drinking three bowls of our wine."

❷   Wu Song entered the restaurant and after drinking one bowl of wine he felt that the wine was very good. He ordered two catty of beef to be eaten with the wine. However, after Wu Song had finished three bowls of wine the owner of the restaurant refused to serve him anymore wine. He said that an average person would be drunk after having three bowls of his wine and would not be able to make it over the hill. But Wu Song was too confident of his large wine-drinking capacity to act according to the drinking limit. Consequently he drank 18 bowls of wine altogether. He paid and picked up the stick that he always carried with him, and when he was just about to step out of the door, the restaurant owner hurriedly told him that there was a tiger on that hill and it had injured 20 to 30 people. The government had already issued a notice. Therefore people should go over the hill in a group. Wu Song had grown up in the neighborhood. When he was small he had gone over the hill many times. He had never heard of tigers on the hill. He would not listen to the advice of the restaurant owner and strode toward the hill.

❸ 到了山下，武松见大树刮去树皮，写了老虎伤人的字，武松想：这是店主人搞鬼³吓人。再走了半里路，他见到一间破庙，墙上贴了政府告示，武松才知道真的有老虎，他怕店主人笑话，不愿回头，想了一阵，还是大着胆往前走。走得热起来，这时酒又涌上来，武松见树林边有一块大石，正想

tǎng xia shuìjiào shùlín li tūrán tiào chu yī zhī lǎohǔ
躺 下 睡觉，树林 里 突然 跳 出 一 只 老虎。

Wǔ Sōng yī jīng jiǔ dōu biàn chéng lěnghàn mào chulai
④ 武 松 一 惊，酒 都 变 成 冷汗 冒 出来。

Tā liánmáng cóng shí shang fānshēn ná qi bàng duǒ zài shí
他 连忙 从 石 上 翻身，拿 起 棒，躲 在 石

páng È hǔ jiàn le rén měng pū guolai bèi Wǔ Sōng
旁。 饿 虎 见 了 人，猛 扑 过来，被 武 松

duǒ guo Wǔ Sōng chéng zhe lǎohǔ zhuǎn shēn lìjí jǔ qi
躲 过。 武 松 乘 着 老虎 转 身，立即 举 起

bàng yòng jìn qìlì xiàng hǔ tóu dǎ xiaqu zhǐ tīngjian yī
棒，用 尽 气力 向 虎 头 打 下去，只 听见 一

shēng xiǎng yī duī shùzhī lián yè diē xialai bàng yě duàn
声 响，一 堆 树枝 连 叶 跌 下来，棒 也 断

chéng liǎng duàn Wǔ Sōng diū diào duàn bàng liǎng zhī shǒu jiū
成 两 段。 武 松 丢 掉 断 棒，两 只 手 揪

zhe hǔ tóu shǐ jìn wǎng xià àn yīmiàn yòng jiǎo luàn tī
着 虎 头，使 劲 往 下 按，一面 用 脚 乱 踢

hǔ tóu Lǎohǔ pīnmìng zhēngzhá liǎng zhuǎ zài dì shang wā
虎 头。 老虎 拼命 挣扎，两 爪 在 地 上 挖

chu liǎng gè níkēng Wǔ
出 两 个 泥坑。 武

Sōng jiàn lǎohǔ yǒu diǎn
松 见 老虎 有 点

pílèi cái gǎn chōu chu
疲累，才 敢 抽 出

yī zhī shǒu tí qi
一 只 手，提 起

quántou pīnmìng dǎ dǎ
拳头 拼命 打，打

de lǎohǔ mǎn liǎn shì
得 老虎 满 脸 是

A stage photo of Wu Song killing a tiger with his bare hands

血，只会喘气。这时武松才放手，在地
上找到打断的棒，怕老虎不死，又用
棒打了一阵，见老虎气都没有了，才停
下来。正想提老虎下山时，怎么都提不
动，才发觉手脚都软了。

GLOSSARY

3 搞鬼 play a joke on

Translation

❸   When he reached the foot of the hill he saw a large tree, and on an area missing its bark it was written that a tiger had injured people. Wu Song thought that this must be a joke, which the restaurant owner played to scare people. After walking half a mile more he saw an abandoned and half-broken temple, on the wall of which was a government notice. Then Wu Song realized that a tiger really was present on the hill. He did not want to turn back because he was afraid that the restaurant owner would make a laughing stock out of him. After thinking for a while he gathered up more courage and went forward again. The walking made him hot and the alcohol was beginning to show its effect. He saw a large stone beside the forest. When he was just about to lie down to sleep on it a tiger suddenly jumped out from the forest.

❹   Wu Song was greatly shocked by the appearance of the tiger. All the wine had become cold sweat, which was oozing out. He quickly stood up from the stone and picked up his stick, and then he hid beside the stone. Seeing a person, the hungry tiger lunged fiercely at him. Shifting aside Wu Song avoided the lunge. Taking the moment of opportunity that the tiger needed to turn around Wu Song immediately raised his stick to hit the tiger's head with all his strength. He heard a crack. A large bundle of tree branches with leaves fell down from above. The stick too was broken into two pieces. Wu Song threw away the stick and used his two hands to grip the tiger's head, pressing it down while kicking wildly at it. The tiger struggled as if it were losing its life. The two paws dug up two dirt holes on the ground. After seeing some signs of fatigue from the tiger, Wu Song dared to raise one hand as a fist to hit at the tiger as if he were losing his life. By then all the hitting had make the tiger bleed all over its face. It could only breathe heavily. At this time Wu Song dared to loosen his grip on the tiger. He looked and found the broken stick on the ground. He was afraid that the tiger was not dead yet and used his stick to hit the tiger for a while more. He stopped only when he saw that the tiger was not even breathing. He was going to lift up the tiger and carry it down the hill but no matter how hard he tried he could not do it. Then he found out that his hands and legs were limp without any more strength in them.

❺ Wǔ Sōng xiǎng, tiān yě kuài hēi le, wànyī zài yǒu
武 松 想，天 也 快 黑 了，万 一 再 有

yī zhī lǎohǔ chūxiàn, yìngfu bù liǎo, zhǐhǎo yī bù
一 只 老虎 出现，应付 不 了，只好 一 步

yī bù zhēngzhá xià shān。 Zǒu le bàn lǐ lù, hūrán jiàn
一 步 挣扎 下 山。 走 了 半 里 路，忽然 见

cǎocóng li zuānchu⁴ liǎng zhī lǎohǔ, Wǔ Sōng xiǎng: "Zhè xià
草丛 里 钻出⁴ 两 只 老虎，武 松 想："这 下

wán le。" Dìngshén⁵ kàn shí, yuánlái shì pī le hǔpí de
完 了。" 定神⁵ 看 时，原来 是 披 了 虎皮 的

liǎng gè lièrén, Wǔ Sōng bǎ dǎ sǐ lǎohǔ de shì gàosu
两 个 猎人，武 松 把 打 死 老虎 的 事 告诉

tāmen, lièrén jiào chu máifú de xǔduō xiāng rén, dàjiā
他们，猎人 叫 出 埋伏 的 许多 乡 人，大家

tīng le dōu bàn xìn bàn yí suí zhe Wǔ Sōng dào shān shang jiàn
听 了 都 半 信 半 疑 ，随 着 武 松 到 山 上 ，见

lǎohǔ sǐ zài nàli cái xiāngxìn le yúshì gāogāo xìngxìng
老 虎 死 在 那 里 ，才 相 信 了 ，于 是 高 高 兴 兴

bǎ sǐ lǎohǔ tái xià shān pài rén bàogào zhèngfǔ
把 死 老 虎 抬 下 山 ，派 人 报 告 政 府 。

Wǔ Sōng chéng le dàmíng dǐngdǐng de dǎ hǔ yīngxióng
❻ 武 松 成 了 大 名 鼎 鼎 的 打 虎 英 雄 。

GLOSSARY

4 钻出 come out from a hiding place
5 定神 pull oneself together

Translation

❺ Wu Song thought that it was getting dark. If there was another tiger coming out, he would not be able to deal with it. He could only shuffle his way down the hill one step at a time. After walking for half a mile, suddenly two tigers came out from the patches of tall grass. Wu Song thought, "This is going to be the end of my life." When he pulled himself together and looked closely he realized that they were two hunters wrapped up in tiger skins. Wu Song told them how he had killed the tiger. The hunters called to signal a lot of local people to come from their hiding places. After hearing Wu Song's story they had their doubts, believing only half of it. They followed Wu Song up the hill and saw that a tiger had died there. Then they believed him and happily carried the tiger down the hill. A messenger was sent to report it to the government.

❻ Wu Song became a famous hero, who had killed a tiger with his bare hands.

Tigers in China

There are no lions in China. Tigers are the fiercest carnivores there. Originally, tigers and evidence of their existence could be found all over China, from the cold northern regions to the hot southern areas. One hundred years ago tigers could still be found in Hong Kong and were hunted by the colonial British, who took pictures of the dead tigers. Since ancient times in China there have been a lot of stories and artwork related to tigers. There is a saying by Confucius that people fear strict rulings from the government more than they fear tigers because the former is more ferocious. Parents make children's hats and shoes into the shape of a tiger's head, calling them tiger-head hats and tiger-head shoes. They also let children play with tiger-shaped dolls. They hope the tiger image will drive away evil spirits. Artists also like to paint tigers.

There are several reasons for the decrease in the tigers' habitat. They have the habit of living alone. One tiger has to have a small area of the forest as its own habitat. Their birth rate is not very high. With the decrease in natural forests, there are fewer places that tigers can live. Tigers do still exist in China now. In northwestern China there is one tiger species called Dongbei Hu (the Manchurian tiger), and in mid-southern China there is another species called Huanan Hu (the South China tiger). The numbers of these two kinds of tigers are very low. They are endangered species and are protected.

GAMES FOR FUN

1. Which animals have the Chinese character "Lao" as a prefix to their names in Chinese? Please circle the answer(s).

tiger   mouse   lion

rabbit   crane   hawk

2. Which terms for greeting people can have the Chinese character prefix "Lao", even though the person being greeted is not necessarily old.

3. Please outline the face of the tiger.